Lessons in Your Rucksack

The complete TEFL survival guide for

- Newly qualified teachers
- Gap-year travellers
- Language assistants
- Summer school teachers
- Volunteer teachers

A resource book of tips, ideas, activities and ready-made lesson plans for your first year of Teaching English as a Foreign Language.

- The basics of TEFL
- Over 150 classroom ideas
- How to prepare
- What to take with you
- Surviving the first lesson
- Instant lesson plans
- Photocopiable activities
- Tips on finding a job
- Advice from teachers who've done it
- Small enough to pack, big enough to survive!

Don't forget to pack this book!

CONTENTS

INTRODUCTION

Teaching English as a Foreign Language (TEFL) remains one of the best ways to fund travel around the world. And with the people on this planet learning English now outnumbering those who speak the language as their mother tongue, you can virtually be assured of finding work in any country of your choice. More importantly, TEFL is also one of THE most satisfying and rewarding means of financing a life abroad. It brings you into immediate contact with local people, challenges you to communicate and stretches your ingenuity to lengths you wouldn't know you were capable of. But beware! The lure and pleasure of teaching for many people – including this author – turns what begins as a gap year job into a lifelong career.

> **ACRONYMS**
> Once you enter the world of **TEFL** you will suddenly meet a whole list of acronyms like **ELT** (English Language Teaching) which is an umbrella term encompassing **EFL** alongside **ESOL** (English to Speakers of Other Languages). For a longer more comprehensive list see Chapter 13 p.151

How can I teach English if I don't speak their language?
This is the most commonly asked question by anyone thinking of TEFL for the first time.

The question might stem from many people's initial experience of learning a foreign language. For many years the language classroom was about translating words and memorising lists, but in the latter half of the last century it became commonplace to learn a language only using the target language. Nowadays, it's normal to find a teacher of English entering the classroom and speaking English only from day one.

Teaching in this way has all the benefits of immersing the learners in the language. It resembles the experience of a person who has learnt a language by simply living in a foreign country and through trial and error.

For another endorsement of this method talk to those other experts in language learning: children. They just seem to pick it up with nothing to translate to and from. Though older learners don't necessarily learn exactly like children, they do also benefit from lots of repetition of a word and the chance to say it many times.

So in answer to the question, imagine you want to teach the name of an object such as *a pen* without translating it. How would you teach this word? Thought of an answer? Now read on to see if you're right …

...yes, hold up a pen and point at it and say, "pen". And say it again, "pen", "pen", "pen"... Now the students repeat it... "pen, pen, pen".

Without translating it you've just taught the word. You don't even have to be holding the real thing. You could mime writing with it, show a picture or draw it on the board. Whatever way you do it, you've just taught your first word in TEFL.

But it can't be as simple as that...can it?

Well no, not exactly, and of course it's nice if you speak the local language or at least start learning some of the students' own language. Your students will love to know you are struggling with their verbs, nouns, collocations, conjugations, as much as they battle with yours. And trying to learn another language is a great way to help you understand how to teach your own.

At the end of the day you won't find out how to teach or what it's like until the first time you walk in front of the class and say "Hello" and introduce yourself. After that you will discover there's an element of finding out what works and what doesn't. Throughout this book there are tips and there is advice accompanying the classroom activities. Whenever possible I have tried to anticipate the kind of difficulties or questions you might have or issues that may arise out of doing a certain type of classroom activity.

Where should I start looking for a job?

This book is about surviving your first months or year teaching English as a foreign language, but if you still haven't arranged a job or you're just beginning to look, you'll find lists of useful contacts in the back pages of this book, ranging from Internet sites for jobs, recruitment agencies, volunteer organisations and tips on working conditions. For even more detailed information you could also refer to the *Guide to English Language Teaching* (ISBN 1-904549-08-X) also published by Modern English Publishing.

How much can I earn?

This depends on where you want to go and how much you want to be there. If you have a yearning for the deserts of Africa then volunteer work may be the only way to go. Teaching in central Tokyo can earn you a high salary but this will cover the high cost of living. What you can't do is compare it to salaries in your own country. As a general benchmark, the cost of renting somewhere to live should be around a quarter to a third of your monthly take-home pay.

MORE IDEAS FOR JOB HUNTING

When writing this book I talked to many teachers about their first experiences as novice EFL teachers. Many of their ideas, tips and words of advice can be found amongst these pages. Some of them began by explaining how they found, or fell into, their first job.

"I was recruited in the UK from an advert in *The Guardian Education Supplement.*"

"I was a language assistant at a very traditional secondary school during my year out on a French degree. My college organised it."

"I responded to a poster for volunteer language assistants on display at my local college."

"I walked into a school 2 days after arriving in Brazil and they gave me a job starting 5 days later."

"Through a company which organised teaching projects."

"We were cycling through a village and the headmaster of the local school invited us in. We stayed for two weeks."

"I sent my CV to all the language schools in Toulouse and followed up with phone calls. They asked me to come in for an interview at the beginning of September and I was offered a temporary contract at first which was then changed to a permanent one."

"Through a friend who was leaving the country and needed to pass the job on."

"I was travelling through northern Thailand and a taxi driver asked me to help out at the local village school."

"Found it on the internet, sent CV, got job – it's so easy to find a job in China!"

"Happened to be in the right place at the right time, an accident."

What training or advice is available before I leave?

You will find teaching posts which require no formal training. Sometimes a degree is enough or the employer will provide training on arrival. On programmes where you work as a language assistant (often offered on university language degrees) you will usually be working alongside an experienced teacher.

There are also a variety of TEFL courses on the market but two stand out as being recognised by most employers around the world: Trinity College London Cert. TESOL (Certificate in Teaching English to Speakers of Other Languages) and RSA Cambridge CELTA (Certificate in English Language Teaching to Adults). Courses leading to these qualifications last at least a month full-time and include teaching practice.

OK, got the job, got my ticket, what should I pack?

Chapter 2 of this book is all about how to use the contents of your rucksack to teach English. It also provides you with a useful list of items to take with you. However, it's also useful to take some resources for teaching so try to make room for the following:

- Blu-tac
- Pair of scissors
- Sellotape
- Correction fluid
- Pictures of your family, friends and home town
- Dice
- A ball (tennis ball sized)
- Coloured pens and paper
- Playing cards
- Photocopies of the photocopiable activities in this book

A NOTE ON PHOTOCOPIES

This book also contains pages to photocopy. If you aren't sure whether you will have access to a photocopier, you might want to make a few copies of each before you leave. At least they give you some classroom activities on arrival so you won't be caught out.

If you don't have access to a photocopier or can't afford to make copies don't worry – just draw it on the board, the wall, in the sand or anywhere so that students can copy it down.

Anything else?

Yes. You need to pack this book. This book is a collection of practical ideas to help you teach – and more importantly – survive those first early lessons. Imagine a cookery book that gives you recipes and then advises you on a complete three course meal – well this book gives you lots of ideas for the classroom and then ties some of them together in Chapter 10. As you'd expect with a good cookery book it gives tips on making your lessons better and becoming a more accomplished teacher. You'll also find comments from teachers recalling their early experiences of teaching and how they survived their gap years doing TEFL.

What about the level of my students?

Students will have different levels of English and you'll need to find out from the school you're working at what level they are. Schools have different descriptions of students' levels but most schools and course books use the terms elementary (or false beginners), intermediate and advanced. Within the term intermediate you may also hear the sub-groups pre-intermediate and upper intermediate.

> **COMPLETE BEGINNERS**
> If you're teaching complete beginners you might like to look at lesson plan 10.2 in Chapter 10 for an idea of how to go about this.

To help you select suitable lesson activities from this book you'll find them graded for levels using the following system of symbols. See the index, p184, for a complete list of all the activities in this book.

■ Beginner/Elementary

This activity will work with students who are just starting to learn English. They can already give basic personal information like their name, age and where they come from. They may know numbers from 1 to 100.

■ ■ Pre-intermediate

This activity will work with students at elementary level or above. Students at this level can answer basic personal questions, describe their hobbies and indicate preferences (e.g. I'd like…). They can form some basic questions.

■ ■ ■ Intermediate

You can use this activity with students at this level and above. Students are now really starting to express themselves, ask lots of questions, give opinions and talk about the past, present or future even if they do still make plenty of mistakes.

Upper Intermediate/Advanced

Students at this level can carry on lengthy conversations. They'll ask you questions and want to discuss complex issues. They'll probably enjoy trying to read authentic texts and discuss them afterwards.

Any level

This activity should work with virtually all levels and is easily adapted.

And remember!

The terms elementary, pre-intermediate, intermediate, upper intermediate and advanced are broad terms. Also, note that younger learners (children) are generally grouped by age rather than level. Only teaching the class will really let you get to know your students and find out over time what they are capable of and also what types of learning activities they enjoy.

ACKNOWLEDGEMENTS

I've written the book that I wished I'd had with me when I first travelled round Europe and taught English as a Foreign Language. After interviewing and talking to many novice and experienced teachers, I hope it's the book that they wished they'd packed in their rucksacks. Many of the 150 plus activities in this book I know are original and have come out of lessons I've taught. I'm quite sure that others have been passed down to me from who knows where and are part and parcel of TEFL folklore. In some cases teachers interviewed for this book have suggested an idea and they are credited. My thanks go to them and all the teachers who gave comments on their "first time" experiences for this book. Thanks also to *The Reporter* for permission to use articles. Thanks especially to my fellow teacher trainers and trainee teachers in Cheltenham, to Nic Ridley for being the spark and to Simon Collin for seeing it through. Thanks also to the person who read and lived through this book – many times. To Stacey.

About the author
At around the time the Berlin Wall came down John Hughes packed his rucksack and headed off for a few weeks as a volunteer teacher in Central and Eastern Europe. Over ten years later he finally returned to the UK where he now trains teachers. He has also written books and articles on travel, theatre and teaching English.

You can find out more about the author and email him by visiting www.johnhugheselt.com.

 What did you most enjoy about living in another country? Being in love.
Nicola, on teaching in Brazil

Are you feeling nervous yet?
Start reading Chapter 1 now which begins with advice for dealing with those first lesson jitters and ways to begin teaching English as a foreign language…

Chapter 1

> If you're positive and walk in smiling, 99% of the time you'll get a similar response. The more enthusiastic you are the more they get involved.
>
> Lottie, spending her gap year teaching in India

Here are some of the things that may flash through your head as you begin your first lesson:

> What if they don't understand?
> What if it's too easy?
> What if they don't do what I ask them to?
> What if they walk out of my lesson?

Well, if it's of any reassurance – and it probably isn't much – just remember that these thoughts continue to dog the most experienced teacher beyond the first couple of years. Yes, the stress level drops with growing confidence but the questions still nag at the back of the teacher's mind. And why? Simply because you care that these students enjoy your lesson and learn English. There are plenty of other reasons such as you don't want to look a fool, but essentially you want the classroom to be an enjoyable sociable learning experience, one which should encourage you to ask:

> What if they do understand?
> What if it's just right – even a little difficult and challenging in places?
> What if they come back for more tomorrow or next week?
> What if they start to chat to me after the lesson?
> What if they start asking me for help with their English?

The personal satisfaction from a lesson well taught will always outshine the stress beforehand. Like nothing matching the stress, so too nothing matching the sheer exuberance of teaching. But me talking about it won't convince you. Let's get started. Lesson One.

> In my first job I spent a lot of time in the teacher's room chatting to other teachers. They helped me with my teaching and planning, reassured me and gave me a shoulder to cry on.
>
> Nicola, on her first week teaching

Planning and preparing the first lesson with any class will be helped by running through a checklist of questions that need answers.

- What level are they?
- How old are they?
- How many are there?
- Are they a new group?
- If they are an old group, can I talk to the previous teacher about them?
- What is the aim of the course and the students? Is it for work? For pleasure or interest?
- Where is the classroom?
- Does it have a blackboard or whiteboard?
- If so, does it have chalk or marker pens?
- If not, where do I get chalk or marker pens from? (a store cupboard perhaps?)
- Is there a tape recorder in the classroom?
- What time does the class start?
- How long does the class last?
- Is there a break in the middle of the lesson?
- Will the students expect homework?

It may be that you can't get answers to all of these before day one. In that case don't worry because all the activities in this chapter make no assumptions about the class. The activities also take into account the fact that you may have been told you'll have a class of thirteen students aged between twenty and thirty-five only to find you are teaching a group of twenty students aged fourteen and under. In other words they are activities that will work with any age group, virtually any class size and with a little adaptation, in any context – from a corrugated tin hut to a businessman's office.

Other questions you might ask could be about access to photocopiers, video players, teacher resources, library usage, computers and internet. You could also ask about whether you have a course book to follow and this is important, but it's a good idea not to use the course book in the first lesson for a couple of reasons: One is that students often haven't had time to get the textbook for the first day or they may have to change class anyway. The second is that you want lesson one to be a social affair; it's about getting to know the students and them getting to know you. If you begin with, "Good morning class, my name's John and can you open your books at page number one?" the lesson may not kick off with the bang you are hoping for.

We'll return to the subject of course books at the end of this chapter. For now we are interested in two things: The first lesson and your survival.

> My worst moment was meeting our Polish host for the first time and being told that the one qualified teacher who was due to join us would not be. As the most senior (only in age) and with very limited experience I was regarded as 'the person in charge'!!! My number one tip for any new teacher of English in a similar situation would be to stay calm and make use of all the resources (especially human) that are available to you.
>
> Paul, a volunteer teacher in Poland

1.1 LEARNING EVERYONE'S NAME

A tried and tested opener for learning everyone's name on day one is to stand in a circle.

1 Hold a small ball (a tennis ball) and throw it. As you throw it you say your first name.
2 The person who catches it throws it to another person and says their first name. This continues until everyone has said their name a number of times.
3 Start again but this time pick someone, throw the ball to them and say their name. This now continues with people trying to remember each other's names.

> The first few lessons were the worst. An uphill learning curve. I realised no-one understood me but I learnt how simple my language had to be ... my number one tip is to be patient, adaptable. Don't have too many expectations.
>
> Gayle, a language assistant with elementary level children in Japan

1.2 BALL THROWING VARIATIONS

Activity 1.1 can be extended in a number of ways. Here are some variations:

Variation 1

With beginners, the ball throwing activity allows you to introduce new language and then let students practise and repeat it. So you can introduce the phrase, "My name's..." when you throw the ball and say your name. The receiver repeats the phrase inserting his or her name and so on.

> **PERSEVERANCE**
> When students don't appear to understand what you want them to do first time it doesn't mean it's a bad idea. Repeat the process and try again. Choose another student if necessary who might have understood what you want to happen.

Variation 2

With higher levels you can throw the ball and ask the person receiving the ball a question; e.g. "Where are you from?" or "What's your favourite colour?"

They then throw and ask the same or different questions.

Variation 3

Later on you can re-use the activity to practise counting, saying the alphabet, revising the names of fruit and vegetables – the possibilities are endless.

1.3 NAME TAGS

The sooner you – the teacher – learn everyone's name the better. With large classes this is especially difficult so creating name tags will help.

1 Students take a piece of A4 paper or card and fold it lengthways in the middle. As you give these instructions hold a piece of paper up yourself and fold it.
2 On one side students should write their name and place it in front of them on the desk. This acts as a name tag which students can bring for the next couple of classes until you're familiar with their names.
3 As an extension activity students could add information to the name tag such as their favourite hobby or the thing they hate the most. Another variation is to have students fill in name tags for their partner. They interview their partner and write the information on the name tag for them.

CLASSROOM LANGUAGE AND INSTRUCTIONS

Give your instructions for activities in a logical order and use short sentences. Where possible demonstrate an activity rather than explain it in words. With lower levels use actions to accompany your instructions. This way students learn the words and have the security of seeing your gestures. Here is a list of useful instruction words with an action given afterwards.

Stand up	Lift your raised palms upwards with arms outstretched.
Sit down	Lower your palms downwards.
Work in pairs	Point at one student with your left hand and the other with the right and bring both hands together. Use a flat hand when pointing. Don't use a finger.
Write	Mime writing with a pen.
Read	Open your hands as if reading a book.
Speak	Raise your hand and move it as if working a puppet – so the thumb is the lower jaw.
Listen	Put your cupped hand behind your ear.
Talk to your partner	Raise both hands and point them at each other moving like mouths.
Stop talking	Put your finger to your lips as if saying "shhh!".
Open your books	Mime turning a page.

In the first few lessons make these gestures very big and clear. After a while they will become natural movements and students will get very used to them.

My best teaching moment was where the students actually stopped me in class and started to ask me questions in English about myself and my country. My number one tip for any new teacher of English is to use your imagination, make sure you speak English and nothing else and make it fun (three tips really).

Clie, teaching in Columbia

▨ ▨ 1.4 INTERVIEW ME

1 Stand at the board and say to students, "You don't know me so ask me some questions."

2 As the students ask you questions don't answer them immediately but write the questions on the board. At first the questions will be straight-forward such as "What's your name?" and "Where are you from?". Students may also be reticent at first asking their new teacher lots of questions. But as they get confident their questions may become more varied. If a student suggests a question with an error, correct it as you write it up onto the board.

SHOULD I BE CORRECTING ERRORS AND MISTAKES?
As this is the first lesson don't worry too much about correcting any mistakes or errors. The aim is for people to get to know each other.

3 When you have between 5 and 15 questions (depending on the level of the group) stop writing. Now answer each question.

4 Ask students to turn to their partner and take turns to interview each other using the questions on the board.

5 If you want the activity to last longer and for more practice with the questions, students change partners and repeat stage 4. At the end you may also need to give students time to copy the questions on the board into their notebooks.

STUDENTS WORKING IN PAIRS
If you have 30 students in a class and they only speak when the teacher speaks to them, then everyone will probably get about 10 seconds each in which to speak. Putting students in pairs to practise is a way to ensure everyone gets lots of speaking time. In some countries you may find students resist working with another student, perhaps because they feel that the best way to learn is only by listening to the teacher. Explain the importance of practice – besides you're not the one who needs to speak English, they do!

If students are reticent about working with a partner, it may also simply be because no teacher has ever asked them to do it before. That's fine. They'll get used to it.

▨ ▨ 1.5 PRESENT ME
As a follow up to the previous activity students present the person they interviewed to the rest of the class using the information they found out. If the class is very

large, students could introduce their partners to another pair of students rather than present them to the entire class.

▪▪▪▪ 1.6 DICE QUESTIONS

For this activity you will need some dice.

1 Put students into pairs or groups of three (or four in large classes) and give each pair/group one dice.

2 Write the following on the board:

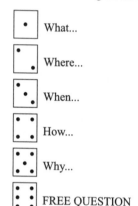

3 One student throws the dice. If the number lands on 3, they must ask their partner or the rest of the group a question using the question word shown on the board next to the face of the dice; e.g. *When is your birthday?* If they throw a six they can ask any question they like. The other students answer and the dice is then passed to another player.

This activity is good for a first class and can also be used later on to review *asking questions*.

> **One thing that always helped me was dice. I used dice to make boring things seem more like a game.**
> Sue, who suggested the last activity, on teaching in Egypt

▪▪▪ 1.7 WHAT'S YOUR FAVOURITE...?

This activity is another way to find out information about the class. It involves students walking round the class so make sure you have plenty of space with tables and chairs out of the way.

1 Each student needs a copy of the survey sheet below. Either make one photocopy per student or draw it on the board and have students copy it onto paper.

2 Students stand up and walk around the room asking each other about their favourites. They write the name of the person interviewed at the top of the column and note down the response to the question; e.g. *What's your favourite sport? What's your favourite song?*

   The photocopiable survey form is designed for six people to be interviewed.

3 When they have finished, students compare their results using phrases like:
   Two of us like football.
   All of us think the bicycle is the best type of transport.
   The bedroom is everyone's favourite room.

BUT MY CLASS IS TOO LARGE FOR THE ACTIVITY…

With large classes divide the students up into smaller groups. If there isn't room to have students walking round the class, then move them into groups around tables, have them sit in circles or simply turn around in their chairs.

WHAT'S YOUR FAVOURITE…?

Sport				
Song				
Actor/actress				
Sports personality				
Book				
Type of transport				
Picture				
Part of your house				

°You may photocopy this survey form.

▨ ▨ 1.8 GAP QUESTIONS

Several of the previous activities have involved students creating questions. Question forms in English provide lots of problems so you might want to give students more practice. This next activity gives students more support with forming questions.

1 Write the following on the board before the lesson begins:
   (a) What's / name?
   (b) / old / you?
   (c) Where / from?
   (d) Do / have / job?
   (e) Are / student?
   (f) What / favourite hobbies?
   (g) How long / studying English?
   (h) Have / ever visited / country?

2 Students must complete the questions with the missing parts indicated by the slash / symbol. They can either write out the questions in full or try to say the questions. (Answers: (a) your (b) How / are (c) are you (d) you / a (e) you a (f) are your (g) have you been (h) you / another)

3 Students take turns with a partner to ask and answer the questions.

4 They could follow this up with activity 1.4.

Variations

You could vary the questions given in stage 1 with more of your own, making them harder for higher levels. Alternatively ask students to think of their own questions and design a similar quiz for their partner by writing the questions on a piece of paper but putting the slash / symbol and missing out certain words.

> ### COPYING
> It isn't always necessary for students to copy everything you write on the board but in many cultures what is written on the board is regarded as important and must be copied. It can be a useful exercise – especially for students whose written script is not similar to English. One compromise is to agree with students that half the board is for things to be copied (like new vocabulary) and half is for things that don't need to be.

1.9 GUESS WHO?

You need a hat (or some kind of container) for this one.

1 Everyone writes one fact about themselves on a piece of paper; e.g. *I have a cat called Tom.*
2 Students fold the pieces of paper up and put them into the hat.
3 Students take turns to draw a piece of paper out of the hat and read it out.
4 The class has to guess who wrote it.

1.10 TRUE OR FALSE

1 On the board write three things about yourself. Two statements should be true and one false. For example:
  ■ **I'm from Great Britain.**
  ■ **I have three dogs.**
  ■ **I like fish and chips for breakfast.**
    Ask the students to guess which is the false statement.
2 Students now do the same, writing three statements. They show their partner who has to guess the false statement. With small classes students could read the statements aloud and the whole class guesses. It could also be a team game where one team scores a point when they guess the false statement read out by a member of the opposing team.

TEAM GAMES
Turning a language activity into a competition, game or quiz where points are scored can quickly increase students' motivation.

1.11 WRITE A PROFILE OF YOUR PARTNER

Following on from some of the previous activities students can write a profile of a fellow student. This could be set for homework and is a useful way for you to assess your students' writing ability. Alternatively, students could write the profile in class and then pin the profiles on the wall. The whole class can then spend some time reading the profiles about each other and learning about the people in their class.

For more writing activities see Chapter 9.

1.12 PHOTO CHAT

Students like to know about their teacher so bring some photographs of you and your family and friends. Show them round the class and talk about them or invite students to ask questions about the pictures; e.g. *How old is your brother? How many rooms does your house have?*

The activity also has a good cultural dimension where students find out a great deal about your country and how people live there. Extend the activity by inviting students to bring in photographs of their families to the next lesson and present them to the class.

> **I wished I'd taken photos of home to help me with my teaching.**
>
> John, travelling and teaching in South East Asia

1.13 COURSE BOOK ORIENTEERING

If you do have a course book to follow, you could use some of the classroom time to guide students around the book so they are aware of all its features.

To do this, write a series of questions where students have to find certain things in the book. Here is an example. You will of course have to adapt the questions below to suit your course book.

1 Where do you find transcripts of the listenings?
2 What page does the grammar rule for the present perfect appear on?
3 Which unit is about "Unusual Hobbies"?
4 How often does a revision test appear?
5 How many units are there in the book?
6 How are the units organised or divided?
7 Which page will teach you vocabulary for talking about the news?
8 Where can you learn more about how to make *Questions*?

SURVIVING THE REST OF THE COURSE

So you survived lesson one! How did it go? Did you have fun? OK maybe not all the time, but you got through and the students seemed like a nice bunch of people. Now you need to cope with the rest of the course. Whether it's a month or a year, here are a few tips for getting on top of things and making your teaching life easier.

1 Planning day to day is fine but also try to sketch out a plan of what you intend to be doing with the students in a month's time or three months' time. This might be a simple list but at least it gives you a focus and a target.

2 If your class is using a course book, spend some useful time flicking through the book getting an idea of what language is taught in later units. Most textbooks also have a teachers' book with ready-made lesson plans and answer keys so make sure you have a copy.

3 Talk to other teachers who are teaching the same level class or who have taught the level before. If a number of teachers are teaching the same level, then create a "study group" of teachers who meet once a week and plan together the week ahead. This is a great way to share ideas and find solidarity.

4 Students will enjoy a systematic approach so introduce routines into your lessons. Have a special slot in the lesson for marking homework or perhaps you can have a mini-vocabulary test in every lesson.

5 On long courses students can prepare a presentation of their favourite hobby, film or book so that every lesson includes a short talk by a student. These regular features are a good way to help you reduce the time you need to spend planning.

Chapter 2

Lessons in your Rucksack

No electricity in your classroom? No textbook to teach from? No blackboard to write on? The one thing in the world you can count on when you first arrive in a new country and a new school is your rucksack. The contents of your rucksack will get you through day-to-day life in a new country and for the English teacher will provide a rich resource of items to help you survive teaching those first few nervy English lessons.

> Take a hot water bottle. It kept me very warm on some of those cold nights. And a hair drier – especially if you have long hair and it is a cold country.
>
> Jane, teaching in -30 degrees

The initial step is to decide on what type of bag to take and how many. The person working for a year as a language assistant in France may see fit to carry two suitcases with room left over for a few luxury extras. The volunteer teaching English for four months in the Andes mountains will probably aim for one compact rucksack containing the bare essentials.

> I recommend you take Marmite! Other things I'd take would be antiseptic kitchen wipes, insect repellent, knickers, bras and shoes if you are going to China and have a big bum, boobs or feet (size 5 is big out there for women).
>
> Jenny, on packing for five months teaching in a Chinese kindergarten

The key to effective and economical packing is to consider how each object you take may have more than one function. Take, for example, a towel. The cult sci-fi book *The Hitchhiker's Guide to the Galaxy* advises that a towel is *the most massively useful thing an interstellar hitchhiker can have. You can wrap it around you for warmth, lie on it, sleep under it, wrap it round your head, wave it in distress, and of course dry yourself off with it (abridged).* As you will discover in this chapter, the usefulness of a towel is extended to the EFL classroom and comes second only in functionality to the all-important dustbin liner.

> Women should take a fly swatter to thwack unwanted amorous male approaches on the street.
>
> Sue, teaching in Egypt

Other than the obvious – clothes and toiletries – here are some of the typical items found in the backpacks of recent gap year EFL teachers:

Swiss army knife	Extra passport	Compass	Sticking plaster
Passport	photos	Mosquito	Travel first
Tinned food	Travel alarm	repellent	aid kit
String	clock	Torch	Bottle of iodine
Guide book	Clothes pegs	Portable iron	(for purifying
Pencil	Maps	Insect repellent	water and for
Tennis ball	Sunglasses	Watch	cuts)
Walkman	Sleeping bag	Toilet roll	Bin liners (for
Newspaper	Compass	Radio	insulation,
Tin opener	Hat	Batteries	wet clothes,
Mug	Sunscreen	Money belt	waterproofing
Ear plugs	Toothbrush	Camera	the inside of
Large T-shirt	Frisbee	Ointment for	your rucksack,
Universal	Bottle of water	cuts	the uses are
sink plug	Box of matches	Bandana	endless)

(Note: don't forget that it's now forbidden to take some of these items listed onto an aeroplane in your hand-luggage – for example: knives, a lighter, or a corkscrew will all be confiscated.)

For the EFL teacher desperate for resources and classroom activities early on the course, all of these items (and virtually anything else you take along) can prove invaluable tools in your English lessons. See also the list of extra items to take for teaching on page ix in the Introduction.

> One thing I wished I'd taken to help me with my teaching was colouring pens and card. My luxury items were a Walkman (for when I felt lonely) and a world service radio too!
>
> Helena, teaching kids in Japan

The following classroom activities will make use of most things that you carry whether it be in a rucksack, backpack, duffel bag, suitcase or shopping trolley.

▨ ▨ ▨ 2.1 GUESS WHAT'S IN MY RUCKSACK

As mentioned in the last chapter, students are interested in their teacher so the contents of your rucksack will provide an initial attention-grabber.

1 Bring your rucksack into class with various items inside – about 15 to 20 items in total. Ask if anyone in the class knows the name of the bag – if not, tell them it's called *a rucksack* and have the whole class repeat the word.
2 Explain that you travel with it and ask the class to suggest items that might be inside. When they guess correctly pull out the item mentioned. If they are not having much success guessing, then give clues; e.g. "it's something you use for …ing." or mime using the object.
3 After five or ten minutes pull out the rest of the items they haven't guessed.

Variation

Add a competitive element to this activity (and for very large classes so everyone is involved) by putting the class into teams of three or four. Tell them they have three minutes to brainstorm and write down all the objects they think might be in the rucksack. At the end show the class what is in your rucksack. The team that guessed the most correct items wins.

▨ ▨ 2.2 TEACH THE VOCABULARY

Not the most inspired activity but necessary and students will want to know the names of any objects they didn't guess if you did the previous activity.

1 Show the class the object, say the word and have the class repeat it. Only plan to present around seven new items amongst items which they already know.
2 Lay the objects out on the floor or table and randomly point at different objects with the class saying the word. Invite students to come up in pairs and test each other.
3 Write the names of the objects on the board for them to copy down.

> ### THERE'S ONLY SO MUCH…
> As a general rule don't introduce more than about seven new words in a lesson as this is considered roughly what the brain can take in at one time. For more ideas on teaching and reviewing vocabulary see Chapters 5 and 11.

2.3 KIM'S GAME

There are different versions of this game but it is a useful way to provide practice with the names of the objects in your rucksack especially with any new words you dealt with in the last activity.

Version 1 – Basic Kim's Game

1 Choose 15 to 20 items and lay them out one by one on the table or floor. You may wish to say the name of each object as you lay it out.
2 Give the class two minutes to memorise the objects in front of them.
3 Cover the objects (perhaps with a towel or bin liner) and ask the group (or teams) to write down the names of as many of the items as they can remember in five minutes.
4 Give one point for each correct item listed.

Version 2 – Flying Kim's game

You need two rucksacks for this version (or use your bin liner). One bag contains the objects. The other is empty.

1 Ask a student to help by holding the empty bag. Stand a few metres apart.
2 Pull out an object, say the name, throw it to the student who puts it into the empty bag.
3 When all the objects have been thrown from one bag to the other students have five minutes to write down what they remember.

Version 3 – Mime Kim's Game

1 Don't show the objects immediately in this version but mime using each one. As you mime, students have to guess the object.
2 When you've mimed all the objects, students try to recall the objects used and check their answers when you bring out each of the objects you mimed.

> OBSERVING OTHERS
> If you're working in a language school, ask to observe more experienced teachers for ideas.

▨ ▨ 2.4 I WENT TO MARKET

This is another way to help students remember the names of the objects.

1 Sit the students in a circle. Put the rucksack in the middle and ask everyone to take out one object and return to their seat with it. You should also take an object.

2 Begin by saying, "I went to market and bought a…". Finish the sentence by saying the name of the object in your hand.

3 The student on your left has to say the sentence. "I went to market and I bought a…..and a….." The student says the name of your object and his own. The next student then repeats the sentence adding the name of her object.

4 This continues round the class until the last student has to list everyone's objects.

5 Tell the students to return the objects to the rucksack. Now you repeat the activity but this time it is done without the objects. Inevitably it gets harder and harder for the students who must list many objects so lots of prompting from other students can be allowed.

6 You can repeat the activity, but let the student who had the longest list of objects to remember start this time. An alternative is to do the game alphabetically. The first student begins by saying something beginning with the letter A; e.g. " I went to market and I bought an apple." The next student must use the letter B; e.g. " I went to market and I bought an apple and a banana." The next student uses the letter C and so on. You can also pick themes such as fruit or vegetables. It's a good way to review vocabulary from previous lessons and a good activity to use at the start of a lesson to warm things up and at the end to round off a lesson. It's also a useful review of the alphabet, which you might need to write on the board.

> For more activities to warm up a lesson or fill spaces when your lesson runs out see Chapter 11.

▨ ▨ ▨ 2.5 A THING FOR …ING

The word *thing* is thought to be one of the most used words in the English language. We use it instead of objects when we can't remember or don't know what they are called or when we are trying to explain something's purpose.

1 Write this sentence on the board: It's a thing for ….ing.

2 Choose an item from your rucksack such as a travel alarm clock. Say the sentence: "It's a thing for telling the time." and ask "What is it?" Hopefully at least one student will say "alarm clock". If not, you'd better go back and repeat some of the earlier activities in this chapter!

3 Continue modelling the activity by passing the clock to a student and having them say, "It's a thing for telling the time. What is it?" to another student who answers. This student then asks the question to another student and so on. You could repeat this stage with a couple more items so that everyone gets the idea.

4 Put the students into small groups. Have one plastic bag per group with 5 or 6 items in. Choose one student in each group to look in the bag and define one of the items using the sentence on the board. The other students must listen and guess which item is being described.

5 The student who guesses first gets the bag next and must describe a different object.

6 The bag is passed round this way until all the objects have been described. Students may describe the same object more than once if it has more than one use (a Swiss-army knife for example). To extend the activity, groups can exchange bags of items and start again.

> ## CIRCLES
> Arranging the whole class (including the desks) into a circle changes the usual layout of many classrooms and, therefore, raises interest in what you are going to do. It involves you and the students on an equal level, creates a team atmosphere and is great for any activities where students must listen closely to each other.

2.6 ALTERNATIVES

The aim of the next activity is to elicit new uses for an object and therefore generate names of other objects.

1 Sit the class in a circle and put an object in the middle.

2 Demonstrate by walking up to the object and mime an alternative way to use it. For example, hold a Walkman to your ear and start talking as if it's a telephone. The first student to call out the word "telephone" goes next.

3 When you have exhausted alternatives with one object, replace it with a new one.

You could extend the previous activity by having students suggest its use rather than what it is. So, for a Walkman used like a telephone, a student might say: "It's a thing for calling people."

> ## DON'T FORGET TO REVIEW
> When you've taught some new vocabulary, don't forget to revise it in your next lesson. You'll find some quick activities to do this in Chapter 11.

■ ■ ■ ■ 2.7 THE SURVIVAL GAME

This is an excellent discussion activity for strong students. It is based on problem-solving activities normally reserved for NASA astronauts or Marines.

> **SQUARES**
> For group or team activities where you want to encourage students to interact, put the desks into squares so the students are all facing each other.

1 Explain that the students have been in an aeroplane crash and have landed in the middle of the desert. They must walk 100 miles to the next town.
2 Lay out 15 objects from your rucksack. Choose ones that are useful for survival (bottle of water, matches, compass) and some that are less obviously useful (bin liner, bandana) and some that are probably no use at all (frisbee, tennis ball). Explain that only seven items can be carried. Which would the class take?
3 Divide the class into teams and allow 20 minutes for each team to discuss which objects they will take. Remind them at the end that they must present their solution to the rest of the class with good reasons to support their arguments.

> **LANGUAGE FOR DISCUSSIONS**
> With discussion activities sometimes students don't speak because they don't know the phrases to give an opinion. It's useful to practise this language beforehand. See activity 3.2 for help.

One variation is to have groups discuss which would be the most important object and the least important and rank the objects in order; e.g. with 15 objects 1 = most important and 15 = least important.

> Brazilians love engaging in any type of role play or discussion activity. They particularly enjoyed the NASA debate where their team is marooned in the desert and they have to choose which items they need to survive.
> Nicola, teaching in Brazil

■ ■ ■ 2.8 IMAGINATIVE ADJECTIVES

A good layout for this activity (and the next few) is to have the class in a circle, if possible, with your rucksack full of interesting objects in the middle. The aim of *Imaginative Adjectives* is to describe an object with many adjectives and to illustrate the order of adjectives. It's useful – and fun – for revising or introducing adjectives.

1 Pick out one object and check the class know its name; e.g. sunglasses.

2 On the board write the order in which adjectives can be said and ask the students to suggest suitable adjectives to describe the sunglasses. Note that certain adjectives won't exist for certain objects. For example, it's difficult to suggest that sunglasses have a shape.

The finished board should look like this:

type / value	size	age	shape	colour	origin	material	noun (object)
expensive	medium sized	modern		black	Italian	plastic	sunglasses

3 Sit down with the group, hold up your sunglasses and say: "These are expensive, medium-sized, modern, black, Italian, plastic sunglasses". Now pick out another object and say a sentence without any adjectives:

"This is a hat."

Ask the student on your right to say the sentence but to add an adjective to describe the material.

"This is a cotton hat."

Then the next student in the circle says the sentence with the hat's origin and the material.

"This is an English cotton hat."

This building up of the sentence around the circle (class) continues until as many adjectives as possible are added to the sentence.

4 The student who completes the sentence starts off the next round with a new object from the middle.

AVOID THE RUSH

With activities that suggest students get out of their seats and walk to the rucksack to help themselves to an object, you need to remember two things: With children it might lead to a chaotic rush. Conversely, in cultures where students are not expected to leave their chairs, you might find a resistance to doing what you ask. Be prepared to have the children come up to the rucksack one by one or hand the objects out yourself to each student.

▨ ▨ ▨ 2.9 MAIL ORDER ADVERTS

Following on from the last activity, students write a short advert for their product.

1 Ask the class to suggest the different parts of a newspaper advert for a product. This might include a picture, a short description, the price and the address or telephone number of the company selling it. Try to find a real newspaper advert to show the students or draw your own on the board.

2 Students can work in pairs or small groups and design an advert for one of the objects. They should try to use some of the adjectives from the last activity.

3 When the adverts are finished, spread them round the room. Students can walk around the room and read the adverts. As a follow-on students can pick an advert they like and write a letter to the company requesting to buy the product.

> For more ways to use the newspaper or magazines in your rucksack see Chapter 6.

▨ ▨ ▨ 2.10 CHAIN STORY

1 As in the last activity, students sit in a circle. Each student picks out one object from the rucksack and returns to their seat.

2 As a class you will create a story. Explain that each person must talk for about a minute. You begin. For example, if you are holding a toothbrush you might start: "I got up this morning and couldn't find my toothbrush. I looked in the bathroom, in the bedroom and finally in the living room. Suddenly, I realised the front door was open. A man was running down the street with my toothbrush. So I…"

3 The student on your right must continue the story mentioning the object he or she is holding. Eventually the story continues round the circle until it reaches you again. The first time the story is told there will be pauses while students think and it may be slow. So, repeat the story again encouraging students to speed up as they become familiar with the plot.

4 Once the story has been told maybe two or three times, tell all the students to stand up and leave their objects on their chairs. Next, they go and sit in another chair and hold the new object. Explain that the story will be repeated so students will have to remember the part of the story involving the object. The student holding your object starts the story.

Variation

For a similar activity but practising writing see 9.2.

> My favourite classroom activity with the students was 'Stories in the round' where you continue a story using a word or phrase taken from a hat. Students loved to tell stories and were remarkably inventive.
>
> Paul, teaching in Poland

> My favourite classroom activity was the story-building element. Every day 10-15 minutes before the end of the class I would get the students around in a circle and I would get them to build a story or to finish a sentence like "When I get up in the morning I...."
>
> Clie, teaching in Columbia

2.11 WHAT AM I WEARING?

If you have no qualms about displaying your clothes in public, then use them to teach the names of clothes. With higher level students you can also teach the names of different patterns, colours and materials (for example: check, plaid, beige, cotton, nylon). Once you have presented this vocabulary here are two of the many ways students practise using it:

1 Sitting in a circle, one student has to pick someone in the group and describe what he or she is wearing; e.g. "She is wearing blue jeans, a red T-shirt and yellow socks..." As soon as the person being described is recognised, a student can call out his/her name. If their guess is correct, it's their turn to describe someone else.

2 This is a variation on the last activity but this time the student who is "it" chooses a person in the group without saying who and the rest of the class must guess the chosen student by asking questions about clothing; e.g. "Is this person wearing...? The student can only answer *yes* or *no*. As soon as a student guesses correctly who is being described, the game starts again.

The last activity also practises the present continuous tense (to be +...ing). See Chapter 7 for more ideas on teaching grammar.

Chapter 3

Conversation Classes and Speaking Activities

Students often feel they know enough grammar or have decided they've spent enough time studying the technical side of language – so much so, they'll possibly know more about English than you. What they really want to do is communicate in English by speaking. The conversation class is a popular choice for many learners as it's a chance to really bring the language alive.

> As I was the only native speaker of English in the school I was given small advanced classes and conversation classes.
> A teacher, on conversation classes in Brazil

You may also find that you can supplement your school wage with private lessons or one-to-one classes where someone approaches you and asks for extra lessons on their own. It might be someone who needs it for their work or the son or daughter of your neighbour who needs help with their school work.

One-to-one often means conversation classes.

> My best teaching moment was doing a one-to-one lesson with a complete starter, who by the end of her 30-hour course could string some sentences together and understand and answer some basic questions. She was very proud of herself and I was too.
> Julia, teaching in France

Having a conversation may sound like easy money but in fact maintaining conversation with a complete stranger for at least an hour twice a week can require substantial pre-planning. Also bear in mind that they will have questions about English and will want some input from you – especially with pronunciation where they will ask you to say a word a number of times so they can get it right.

35

> **FLUENCY AND ACCURACY**
> Getting the sentence right or accurate when speaking is important but communicating a message to another person and getting a meaningful reply is often (though not always) more important to many students. Being fluent in this case is about focusing on communication and so conversation classes will, in general, have an emphasis on fluency over and above the odd inaccuracy. Don't try to correct everything!

The ideas in this chapter will help generate conversation in one-to-one classes and with groups of students and can be incorporated into any lesson where the aim is to get them talking.

3.1 HOT TOPICS

Like going to a gym and beginning with some stretching to get the body ready for some more strenuous exercise, so too students need a warm-up before being involved in extensive conversation. This first activity limbers up the mouth at the start of any conversation class.

1 Before the lesson, write around twenty topics onto twenty pieces of paper. Think about the level and interests of your students and the kind of topics they can talk about. Here's a selection to start off with or choose from:
   - Favourite piece of music
   - A place you dislike
   - Most interesting part of history
   - A painting you always remember
   - Your morning routine
   - A place you love
   - A book that changed you
   - A long journey
   - Organising a party
   - A TV show you often watch
   - A holiday you won't forget
   - Before you go to bed
   - A souvenir from a holiday
   - A room in your house
   - Your journey to school
   - The best part of the day
   - A country you would like to visit

- Someone you admire
- Life in the year 2050
- A famous person you'd like to meet

2 Fold the pieces of paper with the topics on and put them into a hat. If you have a large class, you may need more than one hat or container.

3 Put the students into small groups of three or four. Let one student in the group pick out a topic. The student has one minute to talk on that topic. The other students in the group time the speaker.

4 If the student manages to continue speaking for the full minute they receive one point.

5 The topic must be returned to the hat and then another student in the group picks out a topic and tries to talk on the subject for one minute.

   This activity can be a regular feature of your conversation classes. As long as you keep adding to and renewing the topics it will maintain interest.

I began by asking my conversation class what they were interested in.

Amelia, leading a conversation class with French degree students

3.2 PHRASES POKER

Often when you give a group of students a topic to discuss, the problem is not that they aren't interested in the topic chosen, it's simply that they haven't practised the phrases they need to use. The kinds of phrases which will help discussion are shown on page 38.

Never get Italian students on the subject of food! They're so passionate about it they'll come to blows discussing the subject.

Stacey, teaching in Italy

1 Make one copy of the phrases on page 38 per group of three students. You can have larger groups but you'll need extra copies of the phrases for each group.

2 Cut up the phrases and give one set to each group.

3 The players sit around a table and one player deals out the phrases equally to all the players like dealing a pack of cards.

4 On the board write a series of statements which the groups can discuss such as:

- Computers have made our lives easier.
- The food from my country is the best in the world.
- Global business is good for the world.
- People have too much free time in the 21st century.

5 The group starts to discuss the first statement. As a player speaks he must use a phrase he is holding by placing it in the middle of the table. The player on his right then has to speak using a phrase and playing it in the middle. If a player cannot use an appropriate phrase or uses a phrase incorrectly, he or she must pick the pile of phrases up in the centre and miss a go.

6 The winner is the person who uses all the phrases up first. Then the phrases are dealt again and another topic chosen.

Variation

If you think students will find this task difficult, you could provide more practice beforehand by giving the phrases to pairs of students and asking them to prepare a written dialogue which makes use of all the phrases.

PHRASES POKER

I think...	That's true but...
I don't think...	Yes, but...
What do you think about...?	Definitely!
How do you feel about...?	I don't agree.
I agree.	I also think...
I disagree.	What about...?
You're absolutely right!	On the whole, I agree with...
I'm sorry, I can't agree...	Yes, I think so too.
How about...?	Sorry, but you're wrong!

°You may photocopy this page

WHEN AND HOW TO CORRECT IN CONVERSATION CLASSES

Although students won't want interrupting too much while talking, they will benefit from and probably expect some comments from you afterwards about any mistakes they made (as well as saying how good they are!). One way to deal with this is to make notes of any errors you hear during a conversation. Write an incorrect phrase down or note how someone in the group pronounces a word so it becomes difficult to understand. At the end of the conversation allow five or ten minutes for feedback. Write the errors you noted down on the board. Rather than you correct the errors, ask the group if they can see any errors. Remember that it is much easier to see the mistake when it is written rather than when it is spoken. If no-one can see the error, then you'll need to explain the problem. Keep the error correction stage of your lesson upbeat and friendly. Errors are not bad. They are a sign of learning. Finish off by complimenting students on what they did well.

■ ■ ■ ■ 3.3 START YOUR OWN LANGUAGE SCHOOL

Once you have practised with the phrases in 3.2 you can let the students have a real discussion without the use of the pieces of paper. Here is one way to generate a discussion.

1 Tell the group (or groups) that they are going to start their own language school. They must have a meeting to discuss the following points (write them on the board):

1 What type of student is your school going to be for? (children, adults, graduates, business people)
2 What type of courses will it offer? (short intensive, long, conversation, exam classes)
3 What price(s) will you charge? (expensive, medium, cheap)
4 How will you promote your school? (TV adverts, newspapers, Internet, discounts)

2 Give the groups a time limit (15 – 20 minutes). At the end, one person from each group must present the group's decisions.

If you don't think your students will want to discuss language schools, pick another type of organisation such as a club or business venture.

> **RECORD YOUR LESSON**
> You might find it useful to record your lesson on audio cassette. It's a good way to check that you are not doing too much of the talking. You can also listen to your instructions and think about how they could be clearer. Or listen to your students speaking and think about the kind of difficulties they are having and need help with.

3.4 DESCRIBING PICTURES

1 This one is especially good for lower levels who have less to say in a conversation lesson. Draw a picture on the board like this:

Then write these phrases up next to the picture and ask students to try and describe your picture.

- *In my picture there's a / you can see*
- *in the middle / top right-hand corner*
- *on the right / left*
- *at the top / bottom*

2 Students now draw their own line picture. (Kids might enjoy colouring the picture as well.) You can suggest a theme like *town and country*. Preferably pick a topic you have been looking at recently.

3 In pairs, the students take it in turns to describe their pictures to each other. The listening student must try to draw the picture described. When they have finished, the students compare their originals and copies.

(I first saw this activity at a workshop by Tessa Woodward.)

> See activity 7.9 for a similar picture dictation.

3.5 TELEPHONE ROLE-PLAYS

Role-plays are easy to design, fun and great for speaking practice and conversational skills. And a role-play can be just about anything. To practise an everyday language situation like booking a flight, you need to give students the most important expressions, put them into pairs and have one student playing the part of the customer and the other acting as the travel agent.

> My favourite classroom activity with the students was role-play but my worst teaching moment was when I asked a class to imagine that they were describing something to someone who came from Outer Mongolia and one of the students put up their hand to say that he did come from Outer Mongolia.
>
> Mary, teaching in London

The role-plays here are based around the theme of making telephone calls and are ready-made for your next lesson. If you don't think they'll suit your students, they'll at least give you an idea of how to design your own.

1 Make copies of the role-play cards on page 43 and cut them out.

2 Ask the class what was the last telephone call they made. Was it a call to a friend? To get information? For work? Also check that the class understand the terms *caller* and *receiver*.

3 Put students in pairs. Give each a pair a different pair of role-play cards. One student is the caller and one the receiver.

4 Students role-play the call. When they have finished they can swap *caller/receiver* roles and repeat the role-play.

5 Give each pair a new role-play and continue until they have done all five role-plays.

TIPS FOR SUCCESSFUL ROLE-PLAYS

1 Make sure students know what language they will need to use in the role-play. It may be helpful to write useful phrases on the board. For example, for these telephone role-plays I would write up these expressions to help:
   - *Hello, Can I help you?*
   - *Was that A for Amsterdam?*
   - *I'm sorry, he's not here at the moment.*

2 Give plenty of time for students to read their role-play cards and plan what they will say.

3 Try to make role-plays as authentic as possible. Bring in props. With telephone role-plays sit students back-to-back so they can't see each other's gestures. With role-plays involving students sitting behind a desk (at the train station or tourist information) sit one student behind a table.

TELEPHONE ROLE-PLAYS

Caller
Telephone to speak to Jane Brown. You want to meet her at *Milli's Restaurant* next Wednesday at 12pm.

Receiver
You are Jane Brown's secretary. Jane Brown is not in the office today. Take a message.

Caller
Telephone the train station. Ask for train times to Paris from Berlin. Write the times down.

Receiver
You work at the train station. The trains for Paris leave at 10.15, 12.15, 14.45, 16.39 and 22.04.

Caller
Telephone the holiday company *Travel-Go* for their brochure. Give your name and address: Nicholas Weill, 3 Oxford Street, London W1.

Receiver
You work for the holiday company *Travel-Go*. Write down the caller's name and address and send a brochure.

Caller
Telephone your friend to find out what time the party starts and for directions from the train station to the party.

Receiver
You're having a party. Tell your friend what time it starts and give directions from the train station.

Caller
Telephone the *Hotel Ritz* to book a single room for one night. You will arrive on the 21st June.

Receiver
You work at the *Hotel Ritz*. The hotel is full on the 21st June but there are rooms on the 22nd June.

©You may photocopy this page.

▪▪▪▪ 3.6 ETHICAL DILEMMAS

In this activity students discuss different situations where they must make a decision which may or may not be ethical.

1 Students should work in groups of three or four. Make one copy of the five ethical dilemmas per group. Put the five dilemmas face down on the table in front of the group.
2 One player picks up the top one and reads it out. The groups discuss what they would each do and try to reach a consensus.
3 The next player picks up the next dilemma and reads it out. The activity continues until all five dilemmas have been discussed. At the end, with large classes, each group can tell the rest of the class what they decided for each dilemma.

Variation

1 One person is selected to be "it" and the dilemma is read out.
2 Other players in the group write down what they think this person would do in that situation.
3 Finally, the player says what he/she would do. The rest of the group listen and see if their predictions were correct. A correct prediction scores one point. Other players may challenge the person's answer and try to change his/her mind.

ETHICAL DILEMMAS

You walk into a clothes shop and buy two expensive jumpers. When you leave the shop, you realise that you have also taken a third jumper by mistake which you haven't paid for. You like the third jumper but can't afford it. Do you take the jumper back to the shop?

You're walking down the street and someone in front of you drops their wallet. You pick it up to give back to them but it is full of money. Do you keep it?

In a car park you crash into another parked car and break the left front light. You don't think anyone has seen you. Do you wait for the owner to return or do you drive away?

It's the middle of July. An old friend asks you to lend him money until the end of July when his salary will be paid. You know that your friend is drinking a lot of alcohol and gambling in the evenings. If you give him money, you are worried he will spend it on alcohol and gambling. But your friend also has a wife and two children. What do you do?

You need some more paper at home. In your job you work long hours and receive a low salary. Other people in the office often take envelopes and paper home. What do you do?

°You may photocopy this.

3.7 BOARD GAMES

A board game adds a little bit of competitive spirit to a class and can be designed to help students practise virtually any part of the English language you choose. The example on page 47 is a board game for intermediate students and above to practise the language for attending a party.

1 Photocopy the board game. You can either make one game per two students or for a group of three or four.
2 The students each put a counter on START. They can use small objects for counters like a coin or a key. To move, a player tosses a coin. If it lands on heads, he/she moves one space. If it lands on tails, he/she moves two spaces.
3 When a player lands on a square he/she must perform the task described using language like:
   - *Would you like a drink?*
   - *Have you met...?*
   - *So tell me about...*

Variations

Another board is given on page 48. This board is blank and designed for you to fill in. Make a photocopy and write in prompts around the board including reasons why a student must miss a go. Then make copies of your new version and follow the instructions as before. Like the board game practising language for attending a party, other language situations which would work well include:

- at the restaurant (e.g. ordering starters, complaining to the waiter, asking about the dessert etc.)
- travel (e.g. checking-in at a hotel, asking for train details, booking a flight by phone etc.)

Alternative

You can also do vocabulary reviews with a word written on a space and a student who lands on it must ask another player a question using that word.

> **PRE-TEACH LANGUAGE**
> Try to anticipate new and useful vocabulary for the students. For example, for playing a board game students will need to know words and phrases like:
> *Your turn/go.*
> *Toss the coin.*
> *Heads.*
> *Tails.*
> *Miss a go/turn.*

You fall asleep on the sofa. Miss a go. ↓	Tell someone about something in the news.	Ask someone about their hobbies and free time.	← You forgot to bring the host a present. Miss a go.
Ask the person on your right if you can have another drink.			Offer someone a piece of cake.
Ask someone a question.	*You are invited to my BIRTHDAY party at 3pm on Saturday 25th April*		Ask the person on your left a question.
Ask a player directions to the nearest bus stop.			Ask someone what kind of music they like.
Say what a good party it was and goodbye.			Introduce the person on your left to the person on your right.
FINISH START	Offer the person on your left a drink.	Ask the person on your right a question.	You spill your drink. Miss a go. ↑

°You may photocopy this.

FINISH

START

°You may photocopy this.

▪▪▪▪ 3.8 IMPROVING THE TOWN

1 With the whole class brainstorm ideas for things which improve the lives of the people in a town. If necessary, give examples to get them thinking such as:

- *swimming pool*
- *theatre*
- *youth centre*
- *cinema*
- *old people's home*
- *children's play area*
- *park*

Create a list of about fifteen to twenty ideas on the board.

> ### BRAINSTORMING
> Brainstorming is a technique for making the whole class work together to generate a lot of ideas. Ask the class a question and they call out possible answers while you write their ideas on the board. It's a good way to lead into the topic of your lesson as it gives students time to "tune-in".

2 Put students into groups of three or four. Explain to the groups that they are the local town council. This year is the King's fiftieth birthday. To celebrate you have received one million pounds to build something which will improve your town. You must begin by choosing the five best ideas on the board.

3 The groups discuss and create a shortlist of five ideas. Make sure that they have good reasons for their list.

4 Each group presents its five choices and listens to the ideas of the other groups.

5 Finally the groups meet again and choose one idea and present their choice to the class. End with a class discussion so that one idea is finally chosen by the whole class.

▪▪▪▪ 3.9 BALLOON DEBATE

1 Draw a hot air balloon on the board to check students know what a hot air balloon is and to help understand the concept.

Explain that the balloon is going down. It has four people in the balloon and three must jump out in order to save one of them.

2 Put students into groups of four and tell them to choose one person they admire. It could be a world leader, a celebrity or even just their mother or father. The students imagine they are that person and must prepare a list of reasons why they should stay in the balloon.

3 When students are ready with their notes they must present their arguments to the other people in their group. Set a time limit of around 10-15 minutes. The group of four then discuss who is most important and should not jump.

4 At the end find out if the groups agreed. Don't worry if they didn't. The important thing is that they had plenty of speaking practice.

My best teaching moment was arranging a debate between groups of student to discuss 'the pros and cons of the Polish education system'. This was towards the end of a 3 week course and it was wonderful to see how all the students' confidence in speaking English had developed and how they all became totally engrossed in the debate.

Paul, teaching in Poland

3.10 DISCUSSING A TEXT

The right kind of reading can provoke a good discussion in a class. Look for pages of a newspaper that have opinions expressed and where students can agree or disagree with the views of the writer. The other type of article which is good for generating conversation is one that has results from a survey or findings that might be surprising.

Here is one such article that students may find surprising.

(Note: if you're teaching in a Moslem country, it may not be appropriate to discuss alcohol – why not use the same ideas but with a different text from a local newspaper?)

ONLY A QUARTER LIKE THE TASTE

The English are famous for their pubs and pints so the London magazine "Time Out" did a survey of its readers' drinking habits. Here is what they discovered.

- Bitter is the preferred drink among male respondents (29%), followed by lager (23%).

- London men are three times more likely than women to visit the pub several times a week.

- 56% say they never drink at lunchtimes if they are working. Only 2% drink at lunchtime on a regular basis.

- 81% of respondents to the survey think that pubs, bars and clubs should be allowed to stay open 24-hours-a-day.

- The main reason why people drink alcohol is for social reasons (28%). Many people prefer drinking in public than at a friend's house. Just over a fifth like to use alcohol to chill out and unwind, and a healthy 26% actually like the taste.

Glossary: chill out (slang) = relax, unwind

°You may photocopy this article. Originally appeared in *The Reporter* October 2000

1 Before students read the text, write some brief discussion questions to get them thinking about the topic. They can discuss these in pairs or as a class.
   - Do people drink alcohol in your country?
   - If so, do they drink every day? Once a week? Only on special occasions?
   - Do people drink at home or do they go out? Where?

2 Give a copy of the article to students. One copy between two students is fine as this will encourage students to discuss it. Ask students to read the article and see what it says in response to the questions on the board about the British.

3 Now ask the students these questions to generate a discussion:
   - Do you find the results surprising? Why? Why not?
   - Would they be similar in your country?

4 Ask students to design their own survey. They need to choose a topic such as what people like to eat or clothes they tend to wear. They write their own questions and then ask everyone in the class the questions. At the end they write up the results of their classroom survey as a newspaper article.

For more speaking activities see 1.4, 1.5, 1.6, 1.7, 1.8, 1.12, 2.7, 2.10, 6.2, 6.6, 6.8, 6.11, 6.12, 7.4, 7.8, 7.9, 7.10, 7.11, 7.12, 8.2, 8.5, 8.7, 8.9, 8.10

Chapter 4

Listening Activities

> My number one tip for any new teacher of English in a
> similar situation would be to take along a Walkman
> that you can record on... You can tape music, the BBC
> news or even make your own tape – reading a passage
> from a book, or invent a situation, like a message
> on an answering machine, and record it.
>
> Jane, teaching in Siberia

> My luxury item in Morocco was a good shortwave radio
> to pick up the BBC World Service – a comfort and
> a great teaching aid.
>
> Walter

Listening is often described, alongside reading, as passive. But any learner of a language who has listened feels anything but passive. It takes lots of concentration. Unlike reading, you can't choose when to take a break. Listening also comes top of the list when it comes to the early stages of learning to speak.

You need to hear examples of speech and pronunciation before you can attempt to speak. Children around the world get many months of parents talking to them in the pram so no wonder they suddenly decide one day that they've heard enough and can have a go themselves. Our students also need to listen and many theories of teaching English suggest that lots of listening at lower levels is top of the list in importance. Students will often remark that listening is difficult and they want more practice time.

▪▪▪ 4.1 HOW MANY WORDS?

Italian students say that English speakers *mangiano le parole* or *eat words*. Languages like Italian pronounce the words and sentences as they are written. English is made harder to listen to not only because we don't spell words as we say them but also because we happily squash words together and miss sounds out altogether; for example, "What are you doing?" becomes "Wotcha doin'?" Whenever you are going to teach some phrases or want to warm students up to listening, the following activity can help.

> I finally realised how difficult listening was for students when I asked, 'What time do you get up?' and a student said 'What's a tup?'
> Stacey in Italy

Read out a selection of sentences at normal speed and students call out how many words they hear. Here are some good sentences to use. They are written both how they might be said at natural speed and how they are written fully. The number in brackets indicates how many words are used; note that a contracted form like *I'm* or *you're* counts as one word.

Wotcha doing? – What are you doing? (4)
Where y'going? – Where are you going? (4)
S'gonna be a sunny day – It's going to be a sunny day (7)
Can you tell'em I called? – Can you tell them I called? (6)
Wotsee doing here? – What is he doing here? (5)
Wheresee gone? – Where has he gone? 4)
I haven't seenim – I haven't seen him. (5)
Lemmy spellit. – Let me spell it. (4)

Variation

Read out the sentences at natural speed and students have to write out the sentence in full. This is a good warmer for doing dictations which are described next.

> For more work on pronunciation also see 2.11, 5.1, 5.8, 5.12

4.2 DICTATIONS

Basically, a dictation is simply the teacher (or someone) reading out a piece of written text and students writing down what they hear. The text could be the first few lines of a newspaper article, a verse of a song, even the instructions to another activity. It's useful since it practises writing and speaking as well as listening. If you include language that you've recently taught in a dictation, it is also a good way to evaluate whether students have learnt it.

As a general rule, the first time you read the text, read it at natural speed. The second time, extend pauses in natural places such as at full-stops and commas.

The third time, read it again at natural speed. At the end, hand out the printed version or ask students to read back what they have and you write it on the board.

4.3 GROUP DICTATIONS

1 Put students into groups of three or four. Explain that you will dictate a text and the whole group must write down what you say. They need to discuss how they will do this. It is useful for example to have one student note down the end or middle of the sentence while someone else concentrates on the first part.
2 Read the text once and then let the group discuss what they heard and try to piece the text together.
3 Read the text again, allow the groups to discuss and read again if necessary. The group with a complete text is the winner.

4.4 THE HUMAN TAPE RECORDER

1 Draw the symbols for the controls on a tape recorder on the board:

2 Teach the students the words for each control:
   - *Re-wind*
   - *Stop*
   - *Play*
   - *Fast forward*
3 Read the dictation as normal, but this time students can shout out commands to control your speech. So, if a student wants to hear a sentence again, they shout, "Stop! Rewind!" You read the sentence backwards and they shout "Stop! Play!" in order to let you continue reading.

   (This idea was originally shown to me by Peter Moor.)

Dictation can also be set up with one student dictating to another. Find out how with activities 3.4 and 8.7.

4.5 SIMON SAYS
This is a famous children's game where students listen to you calling out actions and moves. It is good for learning parts of the body.

> **YOUNGER LEARNERS**
> Young children are still learning their own language so their reading and writing skills will not be as advanced as their listening and speaking. So do lots of speaking type activities; e.g. songs (with actions) such as "Old Macdonald Had A Farm". For some more activities with younger learners see Chapter 8.

1 Explain to students that when Simon says something they must do it. If Simon doesn't say it, they shouldn't move. If they do they are out.

2 Call out a series of instructions. For example

Simon says, *"Touch your nose."*

Simon says, *"Touch your right knee."*

Simon says, *"Touch your left toe."*

"Touch your forehead."

Any students who do the last action are out because Simon didn't say it.

3 Call out another series of instructions from Simon and try to catch more students out. The winning student is the last remaining one in the game. With confident classes ask some of the students to lead the game.

Variations

'Simon says' doesn't just have to be about the body. You could do parts of the room (Simon says "Point to the window/door/floor"), objects (Simon says, "Pick up a pen") or students could do it in pairs or small groups.

One thing that I took which really helped me through the teaching was tapes of children's action songs. Doing songs with actions and chants seemed to work much better than learning English without music.
Helena, teachings kids in Japan

4.6 AEROBICS

For more practice with body parts and words like *lift, jump, shake* you can do some aerobics. It's a good way to start a class and get everyone in the mood or a useful technique to reduce the energy levels of over-exuberant kids and teenagers.

Play some lively music on a tape recorder that you can move to like an aerobics class. Start to shout out movements like: "Lift your left hand, up and down...now your right...now both hands....up and down....now your left leg...up and down....and the right...".

It's worthwhile preparing your routine beforehand a little. Pre-teach the words by explaining the actions and movements first without the music.

Variation

Students could come to the next class with their own aerobics routine to try out on each other.

▓ ▓ 4.7 CAN YOU TELL ME THE WAY TO...?

To practise language such as *"turn left/right, go straight ahead, stop"* bring in a few scarves to use as blindfolds.

Each student has a partner. One student puts a blindfold on. The other student guides the partner round the classroom (or outside into an open space if you can) by giving instructions. To liven things up you can rearrange the furniture like an obstacle course.

For more practice with giving directions see activity 8.8.

▓ ▓ 4.8 LISTEN FOR YOUR WORD

Choose a listening where words are often repeated. Typically this could be a song, a poem or a story. Each student is allocated a word from the text. Play the listening or read out the text. Whenever a student hears "their" word they stand up. The activity is a lively warmer and makes students listen closely. For example, in the song "She'll be coming round the mountain when she comes" you would allocate the words *she, round, mountain, when, comes.*

Listening to songs

One reason for the phenomenal spread of English round the world is music and the fact that so much popular music is sung in English. Younger students enjoy music and if you have taken your Walkman with you abroad and some CDs or cassettes, you have an instant resource of classroom material. Students also like to bring in their own music so they may be able to lend you songs to use in class. As you will want to use the lyrics, it's helpful to have the cover from a cassette or CD which has the words. If not, there are some excellent websites on the Internet which provide the lyrics to most songs. Go to a search engine and type in "SONG LYRICS" to find a good selection of sites.

For websites with more classroom material ideas see page 179.

4.9 HOW DOES THE SONG MAKE YOU FEEL?

Before asking students to listen intensively to lyrics, let them enjoy some music and respond to it.

1 Write a series of adjectives on the board:
- happy
- sad
- angry
- excited
- nervous

2 Play a selection of different songs. Students write the name of the song next to each adjective. Afterwards discuss as a class (or in groups) how the songs made people feel.

This is a good way to start off a class using songs and to find out what kind of music your students like listening to and why.

> One thing that really helped me through my first teaching job was a tape of Beatles songs.
> Pete, teaching in the Czech Republic

4.10 GAP FILL
Copy the lyrics of a song and remove every seventh word. Number each gap. Give a copy of the lyrics to students. They listen to the song and guess what the missing words are; e.g.

She'll be coming round the mountain (1)_____ she comes
She'll be riding(2) _____ white horses when she comes...

Variation
Instead of removing every seventh word, remove just the verbs, nouns or words that rhyme.

SONGS IN THE CLASSROOM
As a general rule, play the song once so students get used to it, play it again for students to complete or check the answers they've put, and play the song one more time so everyone understands the lyrics and can sing along!

4.11 CUT UP VERSES

Make enough copies of the lyrics for each pair of students. Cut up the lyrics by verses or every two or three lines of the song. Put students in pairs and give them a set of cut-up lyrics. They read through and try to arrange the lyrics in order. Then they check their answer by listening to the song.

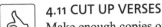 4.12 WRONG WORD LYRICS

To make students listen really intensively, choose some of the most clearly sung lyrics and change the words for another word; for example:

She'll be coming round the supermarket when she comes
She'll be riding six white motorbikes when she comes...

Play the song twice. The first time, students cross out the incorrect word. The second time, they listen for the correct word.

4.13 WRITE OUT THE LYRICS

Asking students to choose their favourite song, listen to it and write out the lyrics is probably something to give for homework. It's excellent listening practice and a task that music fans will enjoy. They can bring their lyrics to the next lesson, let their friends read them or talk about what they think the song really means. Make sure you get a copy of the songs and their lyrics from the students which you can turn into classroom listening exercises. Each student will really enjoy hearing their favourite song being used to learn English and you'll have lots of teaching materials.

> **HOMEWORK**
> Find out if the school you work for has a policy on homework. How much are you supposed to give a week? Although the stereotype image is of students avoiding homework, you may often find that students actually want homework. If you do give homework, be very clear about what you expect (number of words, pages, whether it will be handed in or marked in class). And don't forget to mark it. The biggest demotivator for a student is when the teacher forgets to acknowledge the hours spent preparing a piece of homework.

Listening to tapes

There are plenty of listenings commercially available on cassette and CD. Normally listenings accompany a textbook and have the tapescript and exercises included. However it is easy to make your own tapes before leaving home for free and with authentic recordings.

One simple technique is to ask three people you know (friends and family) to each talk for a minute or two on a topic. Here are some good topics:

- ways you learnt a language or words
- morning routines
- favourite hobby or sport
- my last holiday
- describe what you eat for breakfast

For more topics see the list of 'Hot Topics' in 3.1.

Transcribe the recordings so you have a copy of the tapescript. Ideally this transcription is done on a computer so you can easily edit the text for any exercise – assuming that you're going to be working in a place with access to a computer.

Here is a tapescript of a recorded interview about morning routines. Some ideas for exercises then follow.

I get up around...erm..six thirty...well it depends. During the week I get up at six thirty for work but on Saturdays and Sundays a bit later. Maybe eight or something. During the week it's earlier and I have breakfast at about seven. I usually have toast, coffee, sometimes tea. At the weekend, on Sundays, I often cook breakfast – you know, eggs and bacon.

4.14 LISTEN AND COMPLETE

Listening and completing the gaps in a text is very useful way to develop students' ability to listen for specific words. For example, with the text recorded, we could do this to the text:

I get up around...erm..._____...well it depends. During the week I get up at _____ for work but on _____ and _____ a bit later. Maybe _____ or something. During the week it's earlier and I have breakfast at about _____. I usually have toast, coffee, sometimes tea. At the _____, on _____, I often cook breakfast – you know, eggs and bacon.

In this example the teacher has chosen words connected with time and days for the students to listen out for.

4.15 COMPREHENSION QUESTIONS

Students can also listen and answer questions on what they hear. Possible questions for our example listening might be:

- What time does the speaker get up during the week? And at weekends?
- What does he eat for breakfast during the week? And at weekends?

Another way to check students' comprehension of a listening is to have them simply take notes on what they hear. For example, this table is designed for them to take notes rather than specific answers. Students may listen a number of times, building up more information every time:

	Weekdays	Weekends
Getting up?		
Breakfast?		

4.16 FOLLOW ON QUESTIONS

Give students a task that relates to the listening. This will be questions or discussion points; for example:

- Tell your partner about your morning routine. Is it different at the weekend?
- What do you eat for breakfast?

Chapter 5

Vocabulary Puzzles and Games

If you were about to visit a new country where you didn't know the language, which would you prefer: a grammar reference or a dictionary? Probably the latter. Whilst grammar is important, it isn't much use without words, whereas words can be used to communicate meaning even if the grammar goes wrong. For example, the phrase "to want pen, please" will – in most shops around the English-speaking world – result in obtaining a pen.

Here are some ways to present a new word to students:

- Draw it on the board.
- Show a photograph or video.
- Bring in the object itself.
- Give a reading with the word in and students guess it from context.
- Give a definition.
- Translate it.
- Show it on a scale such as boiling, hot, warm, mild, cold, freezing.
- Compare it to its opposite such as cold/hot, boring /interesting…
- Mime it.

Once you have presented some new words and had students repeat and copy them down, you can use the following activities for practising them. If you can't find what you need here, check out the vocabulary index on page 76 at the end of this chapter to direct you to other activities that might do the trick.

> ## DICTIONARIES
> Students often carry bilingual dictionaries that have a translation from English to their own language. In your lessons they may produce these at the first sign of an unknown word. This can be fine but remind students they can also learn a word by guessing its meaning from a reading or even by asking each other. You can also encourage students to buy a good English-English dictionary which will tell them much more about a word than a bilingual dictionary will, such as: how to pronounce a word, what type of word it is (verb, adjective, noun), how to use it in a sentence and if it's part of an idiom.

5.1 DOMINOES

The game of dominoes is a good way to practise vocabulary. The set of dominoes shown on the next page is to help students practise opposites (known as *antonyms*). Cut up one set of dominoes for each group (of three to four players). Each student takes seven dominoes. One player plays a domino and the next student on the left has to add an opposite. When the player plays the domino, they make a sentence using one (or both) of the words. If the player doesn't have a suitable domino, they draw another one from the remaining pile and wait for their next turn. The winner is the person who gets rid of all their dominoes first.

On page 64 you will find a blank set of dominoes for you to copy and design your own dominoes which can be used for any number of vocabulary games. Here are some ideas:

Word stress (See 5.12)

company	o O o	computer	O o	paper	O o o

Rhyming words

said	eye	pie	sea	me	bed

Verb-noun collocations

tennis	make a	mess	do	homework	play

Complete the phrase

for dinner	How do	you do?	Pleased to	meet you.	Thank you

take	good	bad	happy
sad	black	white	excited
bored	pretty	ugly	cold
hot	big	little	kind
mean	start	finish	lose
find	rich	poor	fast
slow	high	low	wet
dry	work	play	large
small	hard	soft	start
stop	warm	cool	up
down	love	hate	day
night	in	out	push
pull	sun	moon	full
empty	girl	boy	give

°You may photocopy this.

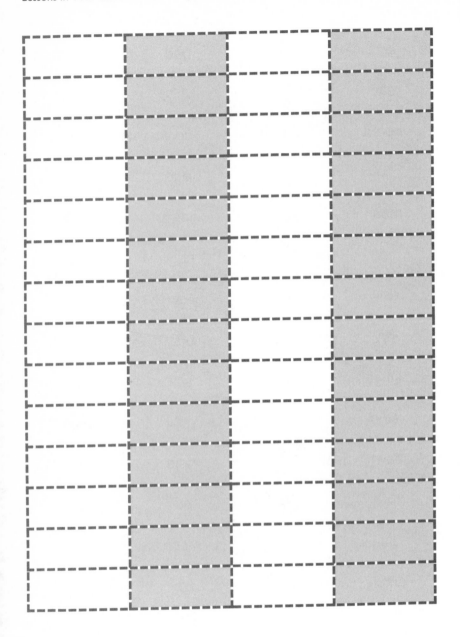

°You may photocopy this.

SOUND AND SPELLING

When you present a new word, students need to say it and see it. Pay special attention to words that are not spelt as they sound – this makes them especially difficult for some students.

5.2 JUMBLED LETTERS

A quick way to revise words you have taught is to write the words on the board with the letters jumbled up. Students must work out what the word is. For example, here are words being revised from a lesson on countries:

1 zilrab	6 yalti
2 crafen	7 rupe
3 regnamy	8 wez nedalan
4 gomnolia	9 janap
5 niaps	10 getyp

(Answers: 1 Brazil, 2 France, 3 Germany, 4 Mongolia, 5 Spain, 6 Italy, 7 Peru, 8 New Zealand, 9 Japan, 10 Egypt)

COMPARING ANSWERS

When students have finished an exercise, you don't have to check through the answers immediately as a class. One idea is to encourage students to compare their answers with a partner or in groups of three. It's a good way for students to help each other and make it clear that language learning isn't a test.

5.3 MISSING LETTERS

Missing letters from words is another good way to review them. In this example of clothes vocabulary, the vowels are missing:

1 Tr_ _s_rs	6 H_t
2 Sw_ _t_r	7 Sc_rf
3 J_ck_t	8 _v_rc_ _t
4 S_cks	9 Sw_mm_ng c_st_m_
5 Sh_rt	10 Dr_ss

(Answers: 1 Trousers, 2 Sweater, 3 Jacket, 4 Socks, 5 Shirt, 6 Hat, 7 Scarf, 8 Overcoat, 9 Swimming costume, 10 Dress)

TO "KNOW" A WORD

"Knowing" a word is to know its meaning, its use (where it goes in a sentence) and how to say and spell it. To check if your students "know" a word, find out if they can say it and write it in a sentence.

5.4 WORD DEFINITIONS

Games which involve students defining a word for other students to guess can be set up in a variety of ways. Here are two of them:

1 Write down recently taught words on pieces of paper. Divide the class into two teams. One player from a team comes and takes a word without showing anyone else. The player defines the word for the team. If the team guesses right, they get two points. If they guess wrong, the other team can guess and win a bonus point.

2 Another way to play is to sit two players from each team with their backs to the board. You write the word on the board and the teams have to try to define the word for the student who cannot see the board. Whichever team guesses first receives one point.

> One technique which I think helped students with their English was a 'What am I?' game where a list of occupations are drawn up and put in a hat. One student picks one out and the others have to ask questions to discover this student's occupation. They can only answer yes or no.
>
> Mary, teaching the vocabulary of jobs

5.5 PICTURE WORDS (MIMING WORDS)

Like the word definitions games, teams can also compete by having to draw the word instead of defining it. One student sees the word and draws it on the board. The team has to guess the word. The same activity can be done with students miming words instead of drawing them.

DRAWING

A quick sketch on the board can answer a myriad of questions, create a context or elicit an answer. You don't have to be Michaelangelo, just practise a little beforehand. Test it on a colleague. Does it get the response you expect?

5.6 SOUNDS AND SPELLING

English spelling is notorious with students because many words are spelt one way but said another. For example, *through, tough* and *thought* all contain the spelling *ough* but all have different pronunciations.

One way to help students cope with this is to have them categorise words into groups according to sound. For example: *through, you, new, true.*

> **WHICH PRONUNCIATION?**
> Always teach students your own pronunciation but be aware that they will hear others. The examples below are based on standard British English but you might say some of them differently – so change them. The important thing is that students are exposed to many types of pronunciations and accents as there are so many varieties of English around the globe.

1 Choose between 12 and 16 words. The words need to be in groups according to the vowel sound they share. For example, three vowel sounds link these words:

> *thought note you taught knew port bought*
> *blue coat through wrote boat*

2 Write the words on the board or dictate them and students write them down.

3 Tell the students to group the words by sound. For example the answer to the words above (in my British English pronunciation) is:

- *thought, taught, port, bought*
- *note, coat, wrote, boat*
- *you, knew, blue, through*

Variations

Students have to spot which word is the odd-one out. Give them four words, one of which has a different sound. For example:

- *caught, walked, worked, sort*
- *won't, want, note, sew*

(Answers: *worked* and *want* are the odd ones)

5.7 BINGO

Bingo is a good way to practise numbers with a class, but you can also use it for teaching words and it doesn't take much preparation.

1 Students divide a page into nine squares like this:

2 Select a topic you have recently been studying in class such as food, clothes or, in the example here, transport. Students think of nine words from the topic to put in each square. For example:

car	lorry	bicycle
plane	train	rollerblades
bus	skateboard	ship

3 You read out a selection of words from the topic and students cross out a word if it is said. When they have three words crossed out either horizontally, vertically or diagonally they shout BINGO!

One of my favourite activities with the children was something called Newspaper Sumo. Two kids stand on a piece of newspaper on the floor. They each have a picture of a sport taped to their back. They have to see the picture on the other person's back and shout out the name of the sport first. They mustn't step off the newspaper.

Gayle, a language assistant in Japan

5.8 CHINESE WHISPERS

1 Divide the class into two teams (or three or more with classes over 20). The teams stand in a long line leading to the board. You stand at the back with a list of recently taught words.

2 Whisper the first word on your list to the students at the back of the teams. They whisper the word to the next person in their team. The word is then whispered down the line until the team member nearest the board writes what they think they heard.

3 This person then runs to the back of the line and you whisper to them the next word which, again, is whispered on up the line.

4 The winning team is the one which puts the most correct words on the board first. They can lose points for incorrect spelling.

5.9 NUMBERS CROSSWORD

You need two copies of the same blank crossword for each student. You could use an unused crossword from a newspaper or copy the ones shown on the next page.

1 In the first crossword students write numbers until all the white squares have numbers.

2 Working in pairs, one student asks his/her partner "What's one across?" or "What's ten down?" The other student reads out his/her number in full (e.g. *Ten thousand three hundred and one)* and this is written down by the interviewing student in his/her second blank crossword.

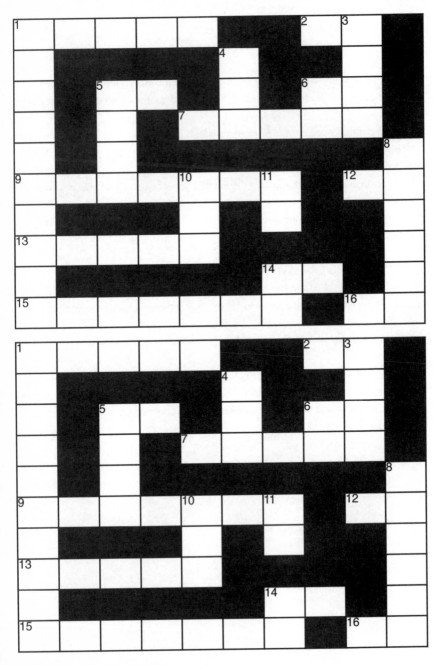

©You may photocopy these crosswords.

5.10 DESIGN A CROSSWORD

Create your own crossword task by preparing a set of clues for words in a crossword, like this:

Across

1 A fruit

4 Me and _____.

Down

2 I _____ football at the weekend.

3 The opposite of *start*.

5 Them and _____.

Variation

Crosswords also make a good "information gap" activity.

1 Make a crossword but design it as two separate crosswords as shown in this example:

STUDENT A

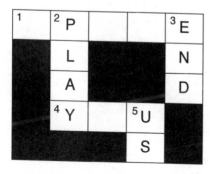

STUDENT B

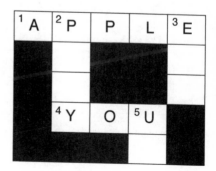

2 Students work in pairs and each receive a different crossword. They ask each other to define the missing words; for example:

A What's one across?

B It's a fruit.

A An apple?

B Yes.

5.11 WORD SEARCH

Word searches are easy to design and children also enjoy making their own. A word search is a box ten squares by ten squares with words written running downwards, upwards, backwards or diagonally. The students put a line through each word as it is found.

Choose words that you have taught recently or that have a theme. In this example the topic is types of fruit: Apple, Pear, Peach, Banana, Tangerine, Grape, Strawberry, Melon, Raisin, Orange.

A	P	P	C	E	T	I	S	K	O
P	G	E	A	N	G	K	T	Z	R
P	E	A	R	I	E	R	R	W	A
L	E	C	A	R	U	T	A	E	N
E	J	H	N	E	A	D	W	P	G
H	Q	U	I	G	O	E	B	O	E
W	O	R	C	N	O	L	E	M	F
A	B	A	N	A	N	A	R	Z	O
E	V	E	I	T	O	R	R	I	N
R	A	I	S	I	N	E	Y	S	O

> **DEMONSTRATE DON'T EXPLAIN**
> In the last exercise you'll see that an example is given. The word APPLE is indicated to show students what is expected. Whenever you give an exercise or explain an activity, it's a good idea to do the first one as an example. If you demonstrate what is required, it will usually be more effective than trying to explain.

5.12 WORD STRESS BOXES

Once you have taught the meaning of a word it's also important to teach students how to pronounce it. You can do this by saying the word and the whole class repeats it. However, it's also useful for students to be able to see how many syllables a word has and know which syllable to stress.

If you have been teaching some words, follow on by having students categorise the words by numbers of syllables and stress. Draw columns on the board and mark the word stress patterns as shown in the example here, which are taken from a class in which the topic was "Spare time". Stressed syllables are marked with a large O and all other syllables marked with a small o. For more examples, see page 62.

O	O o	O o o	o O o
squash	football swimming tennis yoga jogging	exercise badminton	gymnastics aerobics

If you have problems hearing the main stress, hum the word. This helps you hear the main stress. Humming is also a good way to help your students hear the word stress.

> The technique I used that I think helped them most with their English was always asking for explanations of words in English and not getting translations in French. That way they expanded their vocabulary by learning synonyms.
>
> Julia, teaching in Toulouse

▪ ▪ ▪ 5.13 CROSSING ADJECTIVES

To review adjectives, ask students to write the name of a famous person or country on a piece of paper. Using one of the letters in the name they must write an adjective running off it which describes the name; e.g.

```
                E
    M A D O N N A
    U           E
    S           R
    I           G
    C           E
    A           T
    L           I
                C

    S
    C
    E
    N
    I T A L Y
    C       O
            U
            T
            H
            F
            U
            L
```

When they have written one adjective, students swap papers with another student and think of another adjective to add to the name on the paper.

> READING FOR NEW VOCABULARY
> See 6.5 for how to teach vocabulary from a reading.

▨ ▨ 5.14 HOW DO YOU LEARN A WORD?

Encouraging students to think about how they learn words and then learning new ways of doing it is a useful way to help them learn even more.

1 Write this on the board:

I learn a new word by:

- *drawing a picture*
- *writing the definition*
- *translating it*
- *writing a sentence using it*
- *repeating it*

2 Students can either copy it down and tick the ones that are true for them or discuss them with their partner.

3 Students think of two more ways in which they learn vocabulary.

4 Tell the students to stand up and walk around the class telling each other their two ways.

5 At the end, as a class, add the new ideas to the list on the board so everyone can learn about other ways to learn vocabulary.

6 Pick three words and write them on the board. Ask students to choose three different techniques from the board to learn the words and then have them use the techniques; e.g. drawing a picture of it or writing a sentence using the word.

VOCABULARY INDEX

As well as the activities in this chapter, you will find that many of the activities in this book will be helpful for introducing and practising different areas of vocabulary.

Chapter 6

Using Newspapers and Reading Activities

However much the gap-year traveller wants to be immersed in the culture of a country, there are times when you simply need to have contact with home. Receiving news is a great way to stave off the homesick blues, so reading newspapers is one way to transport yourself back to your own culture, even if it's just for an hour or so. Not surprising then that one of the most useful cited presents received by many teachers on leaving home was not yet another travel guide to the country nor another brand of mosquito repellent. It was in fact a year's subscription to a newspaper.

> ### CULTURE SHOCK
> Culture shock is the anxiety you might feel after a few weeks when you first move to a new country. It often follows the honeymoon period of a new life in a new country where you probably feel euphoric and excited by all things new. Culture shock strikes on those days when you are failing to make yourself understood with your limited command of the local language; maybe you've had to suffer some local bureaucracy; perhaps you suddenly have feelings of anger towards the country and develop stereotype views of the culture. For most people it passes and they achieve an acceptance of the country and a sense of belonging. You can deal with the stress of culture shock, loneliness or a longing for home in a variety of ways: take some exercise, travel and visit a new place, learn the language, listen to some music or tune into the World Service. Whatever technique you use, don't spend time worrying that you may not be coping – culture shock is normal and will pass.

Newspapers in the classroom
Your students will also like newspapers and many will want to try to read them in English as a way to improve their language skills and increase their vocabulary.

Newspapers are authentic and provide students with a sense of understanding *real* English – not the English of a textbook or the classroom.

Teachers shy away from using newspapers usually because they think the language will be too difficult. This might be true sometimes, but with a little thought and imagination you can prepare a lesson where students really can interact with some authentic English.

> We used to let them read our English magazines so they picked up English the way it is spoken now instead of the very strange exactly correct colonial English they were taught by the other teachers.
>
> Will, on a volunteer teaching project in Kenya

Access to news

If you've failed to convince relatives or friends to buy you a newspaper or magazine subscription, then buy one yourself. Prices are usually reasonable and many regularly have special offers and discounts on 12-month subscription prices.

Alternatively, you can also buy your favourite newspapers and magazines overseas though this is an expensive option. Obvious places to buy are at airports or mainline train stations. Large hotels often have shops in the reception areas where you can buy them but, again, the prices can be exorbitant. In capital cities you should be able to find a newsagent selling newspapers from all over the globe.

> **NEWSPAPERS ON THE INTERNET**
> Don't forget that many newspaper now have websites where you can read articles and features; visit www.thepaperboy.com for a list.

Also find out if the school you are going to work in has a library or self-access centre. Self-access centres provide students with extra resources to study by themselves and will often include newspapers and magazines in English.

Which to buy?

Buy and use a newspaper which you are interested in reading and which you think your students will find useful. It needs to have broad appeal. It's no good buying a specialist magazine on sport, for example, when it's only you and two other people in the class who are bothered about the football results. Similarly, a gossip magazine is not much use in a country where nobody knows – or cares – where Hollywood is. Here are some of the typical titles available overseas:

The Guardian Weekly – An international weekly version of the UK daily with lots of articles that are relevant to any nationality.

The Week – This is (surprise surprise) a weekly digest of articles and viewpoints from all the different UK newspapers. It tends to choose short articles of a manageable length for learners.

The Economist – Fortnightly, it is an international news and business magazine which can be heavy going but useful if you teach business students.

Newsweek / Time Magazine – competing magazines which round up world news and politics and avoid too much idiomatic language.

The Herald Tribune – a popular newspaper for US citizens living abroad. In some countries it includes supplements on news happening in the country where it is being sold. This means students may have read about the topics in their own language, making it easier to understand the same news in English.

Hello – This is a glitzy, gossipy, celebrity-obsessed magazine. The texts are easy to read and quite low-level students will cope with them. But the most important feature of this type of magazine is the numerous photographs of people, which are especially useful in class. If you can't buy this particular magazine, don't worry. Most countries seem to have their own national equivalent with an endless supply of the grinning and the famous.

Women's magazines – Many of them (*Cosmopolitan* in particular) include questionnaires which students enjoy completing and learning lots of interesting language on the way.

Tabloids – These newspapers can be fun as they often have interesting headlines and the articles tend to be short. But beware! Many are riddled with idioms and puns which are often incomprehensible to anyone not living in the UK.

The vast majority of my students were unmotivated, but having a native speaker teacher of a similar age to them meant that I had loads of cultural information for them. I could talk about things they were interested in or knew what they'd enjoy reading about.

Karen, a language assistant in France

■ ■ ■ 6.1 WHAT DO YOU READ?

The teacher's worst nightmare is to choose an article for students to read and discover that no one in the class (except you) is interested in the subject matter. So, it's useful to begin by finding out what students actually read and then select a relevant piece.

1 Bring in a few copies of English newspapers and hold one of them up for everyone to see. Ask the class to name the parts of a newspaper. Give a couple of examples to get them going; e.g. *sport, weather.*
2 Write their ideas on the board, which will include *world news, domestic news, letters, the arts, comment and analysis, the editorial, book reviews, gossip columnist, crossword,* etc.
3 Hand out one newspaper to each group (no more than four students per group). Ask the groups to find more categories to add to the list on the board by flicking through the paper and studying the contents. This will take some time as students will inevitably get sidetracked looking at the articles, pictures and adverts. It's best to set a time limit (of five minutes or so) and remind them of the task if they start asking you to explain complicated headlines or articles.
4 Ask for any new sections found to be added to the list on the board.
5 Students write down the list on the board and number each category in the order in which they read it. So, if a student reads the sports pages first, they write the number 1 next to it. If they read the world news next, they write 2 next to it. If there is a part they never read, they write 0 next to it. You can illustrate this by numbering the order in which you would read a newspaper so the students see what you expect them to do.
6 When they have finished, they compare their list in small groups. They can explain their answer to the group or to the whole class. Collate their numbers on the board as a grid, so it looks like this:

Sport	1	2	0	
Cartoons	4	3	2	
Letters	0	0	3	
The arts	3	0	1	

From this table students can see what they each read and you can find out what types of newspaper articles will be of interest to use in future lessons.

Variation

With higher-level groups you might also want to encourage a discussion on what the main differences are between English newspapers and newspapers in their country.

> ### TEACHING READING
> There is something odd about the idea of being told how to teach reading. After all, don't we just, ermmm…read? Well yes, but you can help students immensely with the challenging prospect of understanding a newspaper text in a foreign language by breaking down the reading process into parts. First of all encourage students to predict what they will read and then read for the general meaning.

6.2 PREDICTING THE ARTICLE

1 Begin by showing the students only the headline or photograph of your chosen article and ask them to guess what they think the article is about. Encourage any ideas at this stage. If you have to prompt them, here are some questions you could ask the class:

- *Who do you think the person is in the picture?*
- *What will happen next?*
- *Where do you think it is happening?*
- *Why is the person angry/sad/happy etc.?*
- *Who is the person mentioned in the headline?*
- *What part of the paper do you think the headline appears in? Sport? News?*
- *Have you read a similar headline (or seen a similar photograph) in your newspaper today?*

2 Hand out the article and let students read it to see if their predictions were correct. At this stage students may find words they don't understand. Tell them not to worry and say that you will be teaching these words later on in the lesson. The aim here is that students understand the main meaning of the text – not every word.

In one of my first lessons I chose a film review of 'Billy Elliot'. We had a conversation about it and then watched the video.
Amelia, a language assistant

▨▨▨▨ 6.3 SCANNING

1 To help students understand the main points of the article, write some key facts from the text on the board or read them out and students write them down. For example, if it is an article with lots of figures and numbers, write them up on the board or dictate them and students write them down.

2 Hand out the article and students find out what the dictated facts/figures refer to. This can be done as a race with students competing to find the information first.

> ### YOU DON'T NEED TO UNDERSTAND EVERY WORD
> For some activities (such as 6.3) students don't need to understand every word in the article to complete the task. If students get caught up on one word, you might try to explain it but often it's worth encouraging them to move on.

▨▨▨▨ 6.4 TRUE/FALSE STATEMENTS

One way to check students' initial understanding of the article is to use True/False statements. Prepare a series of statements that summarise parts of the article. In some cases change the statement so it is false. Write the statements on the board and ask students to mark them *True* or *False*.

Here are some examples for the reading on page 136 activity 10.7 which you can use with your own students.

Are these statements True or False? Mark them T or F.

(a) Scientists believe the word *mother* was the first word ever spoken.

(b) Babies in any country produce similar sounds.

(c) Adults copy the language of babies.

(d) Babies produce consonants more easily than vowels.

(e) Babies' bodies are not ready to produce real words.

(Answers: (a) F; (b) T; (c) T; (d) F; (e) T)

▨▨▨▨ 6.5 VOCABULARY WORK

Newspaper articles contain many new words so it's a good chance to teach new vocabulary. Here are some techniques you can use:

1 Students find a word in the article that means the same as another word. For example, if the article contained the word *costly* you would write the word *expensive* on the board and students search for the similar word. Seven is a good number of words to do this with. You can use a similar technique for idioms in the text; i.e. *prices go through the roof* could be matched with *prices increase dramatically*.

2 As with the previous technique, choose six or seven new words and write the dictionary definitions of these words on the board. Students must find and match the words from the article to their definitions. You can simplify the activity by underlining the words that have to be matched.

3 Choose seven words and remove them from the text. You can do this with a black marker or correction fluid. If you take the article off the Internet, you can delete the word. Write the erased word on the board or above the article. Students must guess where the missing words go.

> See Chapter 5 and 10.7 for more ideas on teaching vocabulary.

6.6 REACTIONS

If you intend to provoke debate or discussion from an article, it's useful to let students have time to formulate their ideas and views.

1 Take an article that clearly contains both sides of a debate or pick two articles offering different viewpoints on the same issue.

2 When students have read the article, ask them to work by themselves for a few minutes and complete these sentences:

The article surprised me because…

I disagree with the writer because….

I agree with the view that…

I'm not sure about…

I'd like to know more about…

It's difficult to agree or disagree because…

In my opinion…

3 When students have prepared their sentences, ask one or two of them to read their sentences out and ask other students to respond. It's not important that all sentences are read out by everyone, but that the class has prepared the language they need to discuss the issues in the article.

6.7 FEATURES AND INTERVIEWS

Where there is a featured person in the article, students can imagine they are journalists.

1 Students write questions for the personality that are not answered in the article. For example, "Do you like…?", "What do you think about…?", "How long have you been married to…?"

2 When the questions are ready, students can interview each other with one of them pretending to be the person in the article.

3 Students write another article based on the interview.

Variation

You could begin the above activity by first asking students to predict the questions that they think the interview will answer. They write their questions down and then read the text to find the answers.

6.8 SPORTS

The pages in the sports section of newspapers contain many ways to express winning and losing.

1 Collect some headlines with phrases describing who won or lost. Here are some examples:

GERMANY DEAL A BLOW TO SPAIN'S HOPES
FRANCE CRUSHED BY SENEGAL
BRAZIL CRUISE HOME AGAINST TURKEY

2 Students study the headlines and make two lists of phrases for winning or losing, like this:

WINNING	LOSING
deal a blow	crushed by
cruise home against	

3 Now write a series of results on the board. For example:

ITALY 3 IRELAND 1
ARGENTINA 2 COSTA RICA 3

Using the *winning/losing* language collected, students create their own headlines; for example:

ITALY CRUISE HOME AGAINST IRELAND

▦ ▦ ▦ 6.9 NEWS HEADLINES

Headlines are shortened sentences and have various words missing. For this reason they are very useful ready-made gap-fill exercises or sentences. For example, the headline *CLINTON TO MEET MANDELA* is short for *President Clinton is going to meet Nelson Mandela.*

1 Place a pile of headlines in the centre of the class.
2 Students come up and take one headline, return to their desk and write a complete sentence based on the headline.
3 They return the headline and choose another one.
4 After they have written a few sentences, in groups of three, students compare their sentences with each other.

   Remember that students may ask to read the actual articles after the activity so have them standing by.

▦ ▦ ▦ 6.10 OBITUARIES

The obituary page provides mini-biographies of famous people and gives useful practice with the past tense.

> **WEBSITE RESOURCES**
> The website www.biography.com also provides lots of articles on famous people. See page 179 for more useful sites.

1 Dictate the years mentioned in the obituary and students write them down (working in pairs if they want to).
2 Students read the obituary and find out what happened on the dates mentioned.
3 In groups, students design a timeline for the person described. For example, here is a timeline for Elvis Presley:

1935	1945	1954	1958	1969	1977
was born in Tupelo	*won singing contest*	*recorded first single*	*joined army*	*had last No.1 hit*	*Died in Memphis*

4 Ask students to design a timeline for a famous person they know about (or ask them to research it for homework). Each student presents the timeline to the rest of the class.

COPING WITHOUT COPIES

If you have access to a printer or photocopier, it's straightforward to make copies of an article for every student. If you don't have such technological luxuries, here are some ways around the problem.

1 Buy multiple copies of one newspaper so that it can be used many times.

2 Dictate the article to students so that they write it down. Dictation is good for listening and writing and useful even if you have copies for everyone. (See 4.3)

3 Design questions and tasks for different articles. On one day, two or three students work on one article while another group work on a different article. The next day they swap.

4 Set comprehension questions for different articles. Pin the articles up around the room. Students walk around the room from article to article collecting answers. (See 6.4)

5 Cut up the article paragraph by paragraph. Give one paragraph to each student. They read their paragraph and as a group describe what they have read. They try to guess who had the first paragraph, who had the second, the third and so on. The paragraphs are laid out on a table and arranged into their original order. (See 10.7)

6 Build up a library of interesting articles. Paste them onto cards so students can borrow them.

> The school didn't have a photocopier – you had to take a taxi to a local place. There was a small cupboard of books but it was locked, the receptionist held the key and teachers weren't allowed access – mmm that makes sense!
>
> A first-time EFL teacher on photocopiers in China

6.11 FAMILY VIEWING

For a fun way to generate the language of discussion and arguments and to simulate a situation familiar to any student who comes from a family with only one TV in the house, this activity is the one!

1 Ask the class to call out the names of different types of TV programmes and write their ideas on the board. Their responses should include *sport, comedy, news, documentary, film, cartoons, children's TV* and *drama.*

2 Make and hand out one copy of the TV listings page in a newspaper for each student. If it covers many different channels, pick only four such as BBC 1, BBC 2, ITV and Channel 4. Students must find one example of each of the programme types listed on the board. In groups they compare their answers.

3 Divide the class into groups of four. Explain that they all live together in the same house and there is only one TV. Allocate the roles of mother, father, son and daughter. If you have to have groups of five, introduce the character of granddad or grandmother.

4 Each member of the household must now circle all the TV programmes shown in the newspaper that he or she would like to watch.

5 When everyone has chosen their favourite programmes, the family comes together, discusses its choices, and tries to reach an agreement on which programmes will be watched during the day. Allow plenty of time for this and expect that in some cases there may not be a resolution.

6 At the end, each group should present their finalised schedule of viewing to the rest of the class.

6.12 CARTOONS

Take a cartoon story with four or five pictures (e.g. the Peanuts/Charlie Brown cartoons). Cut up the cartoon so that the pictures are not in the correct order. If the cartoon has five pictures, then create a group of five students. Each student gets one picture and takes it in turns to describe his/her cartoon picture without showing it. The group must decide in what order the cartoon should appear.

See 9.9 for another way to adapt a cartoon.

6.13 PORTRAITS

Photographs of people are useful to cut out and keep as they can be used in all sorts of ways in the classroom. The pictures may be of famous people but also of ordinary people in – perhaps – strange or unusual situations. Here are three ways to use pictures of people:

1 Choose pictures of individuals which are easy to describe. Hand out one picture to each student and have them write a description of the person shown. Collect in the pictures and the written descriptions. Place the pictures around the room and hand out the written descriptions randomly to the students. Make sure no student receives his or her own description. Students read the description and walk around the room deciding

which photograph is being described.

2 Give students photographs of famous people and have them write interview questions for that person. (See 6.7)

3 Put students in pairs and give each pair two photographs of two famous people. The students discuss what these two famous people might say to each other if they were to meet. When they have discussed this, the students can role-play the conversation.

Alternative

Find interesting pictures from newspapers where people are talking to each other. Ask students to think of what they think is being said. Ask students to write a conversation based on the picture.

Chapter 7

Introducing Grammar

> My worst teaching moment was trying to teach them English grammar that I didn't even understand myself so I couldn't even answer any of their questions. Eventually I just turned it into a chat about the London Underground.
>
> Will, on volunteer teaching in Kenya

What scares so many teachers is the prospect of teaching grammar. We don't learn our own language by knowing the grammatical terms and how sentences fit together. We don't formally learn our language but somehow acquire it like sponges soaking up water.

As we get older and try to learn other languages we can also acquire a language by picking it up, but to use the sponge analogy again, we can also lose it very quickly if we don't use it.

Another way we learn language as we get older is to categorise the language into grammar. Organising language by grammatical categories is very popular in language teaching but there is a danger that students learn lots of rules and never how to use the language. It's important then to give the grammar a meaningful context so that students can practise the new language item in an authentic way.

As a language assistant or conversation teacher you may find that you never formally teach grammar. However, if you use textbooks you'll discover that many have chapter headings and contents pages based around grammatical terms.

The activities in this chapter are not organised by grammatical headings because like all the other activities in this book you can use them simply to provide more general language practice.

However, if you have a specific grammar lesson to teach, you'll also find they have a sub-heading called Grammar Focus so you can choose an appropriate activity.

If you can't find an activity to suit in this chapter, then you may find another activity in this book that will lend itself to teaching grammar.

GRAMMAR INDEX

To help you find an activity here is a grammar index to this book organised by grammatical terms and possible activities that will practise the form.

Comparatives and superlatives 1.7, 3.2, 7.7
Conditionals 2.7, 3.6, 3.9, 7.11
Countable and uncountable nouns 7.12
Future 7.4, 7.6
Imperatives 3.4, 4.5, 4.6, 4.7, 8.2, 8.9, 9.4, 9.5
Modal verbs 2.7, 7.10, 9.10
Past tenses 1.11, 2.4, 2.10, 3.9, 6.11, 7.5, 7.6, 7.8, 9.1, 9.8
Prepositions of place 7.9
Present continuous 2.12, 7.2, 7.3, 9.7
Present perfect 7.8
Present simple 1.4, 1.5, 1.7, 1.8, 1.9, 1.10, 1.11, 1.12, 3.9, 3.10, 4.13, 7.1, 7.6, 7.8, 8.7 8.16
Question forms 1.4, 1.6, 1.7, 1.8, 1.12, 4.15, 8.5, 8.14

7.1 TRAVEL INFORMATION

Grammar Focus: *The present simple* tense for talking about times

1 Take a timetable such as a train or bus timetable. Make two copies of it, marking one Student A and the other Student B. White out different times on each using correction fluid. (Alternatively, you can use the ready-made photocopiable timetables on the next page.) Make enough copies for each student.

> I flew to Poland and taught numbers and telling the time using my airline ticket stubs during the first week of teaching.
> Stacey, teaching in Poland

2 Students ask each other questions to complete the missing information. For example:
- *What time does the train leave for...?*
- *Which platform does it leave from?*

STUDENT A

	Arrive	Depart	Platform
Gloucester	11.41	———	1
Swindon	———	12.57	———
Reading	13.25	———	3a
London	———	14.08	———

-------------------- cut along this line --------------------

STUDENT B

	Arrive	Depart	Platform
Gloucester	———	11.46	———
Swindon	12.50	———	2
Reading	———	13.30	———
London	14.00	———	14

°You may photocopy this table.

7.2 WHAT AM I DOING?

Grammar Focus: *The present continuous* for an action happening now.
e.g. I am swimming, you are watching TV.

1 Take a selection of pictures from magazines of people doing things into class;
   e.g. playing football, watching TV, walking down the street, etc.
2 Ask one student to come to the front of the class, look at a picture and mime the
   action of the person shown.
3 The class have to guess what he or she is doing. The student who guesses first comes
   up to do the next mime.

> One thing I took that really helped me through my
> teaching was my French-English dictionary which had
> all the English grammar explained in the back.
> Julia, teaching in France

7.3 ARRANGING TO MEET

Grammar Focus: *The present continuous* for an event already arranged
e.g. I'm meeting him at 3pm.

1 Ask students to write the days of the week down the side of a page. Tell them that this is their diary for next week. Next to each day ask them to write something they have arranged to do and the time it is scheduled for; e.g.
   - **Monday**   2pm Dentist
   - **Tuesday**   12pm Meet friend for lunch
   - **Wednesday** 8pm Cinema

2 Put the students in pairs and ask them to arrange to meet next week. As they try to make arrangements they should explain to their partner why they can't meet at certain times. For example:
   - *Can you meet on Tuesday at 12?*
   - *Sorry, I'm meeting a friend for lunch.*

3 When they have arranged to meet one person in the class, they move to another person and try to meet. The more students they meet, the more difficult it will become for an arrangement to be made.

7.4 PREDICTING THE FUTURE

Grammar Focus: *Will* for future, *to be going to..., future perfect*
e.g. you'll meet someone, you're going to be rich, by next year you will have found a new job

1 Draw four squares on the board and tell students to copy the squares onto a piece of paper. The top left hand box represents *future wealth*, the top right represents *love*, the bottom left is *travel* and the bottom right is *achievement*. The finished paper should look like this:

Wealth	Love
Travel	Achievement

2 Put students into pairs and tell them to predict the future of their partner by drawing their future in each box; e.g. you might draw a mystery person in the square marked *Love,* a certificate in the box marked *Achievement,* a picture of France under *Travel.*

3 Students spend time drawing in the four boxes. When the pairs are ready they take turns to ask each other questions about their own future; e.g.
Will I be rich? How rich? Will I own a house? Am I going to live in another country...

4 Once a student has asked questions and guessed correctly about a square, they move on to the next square. At the end the students give each other the four squares so they can see exactly what was drawn.

ELICIT AND PRAISE

Asking students for words or eliciting is a good way to motivate them. Good ways to elicit words are by showing pictures or asking questions; e.g. What are some types of transport? Another way to motivate is to give praise. These phrases will come in useful:

Great.

That's great.

Well done.

Good.

Excellent.

You worked really hard!

7.5 TALKING ABOUT THE PAST

Grammar Focus: *The past simple* for a specific event in the past
e.g. I left school in 1984.

1 Write down five years in your life that have been important to you; e.g. the year you were born, the year you started school, the year you graduated, the year your team won the cup etc. Write these years on the board.

2 Ask students to guess why those years are important using the past simple; e.g.
Student: You were born in 1987?
Teacher: No.
Student: You left university in 1987?
Teacher: Yes.

3 When all five years have been guessed, ask students to write their important five years. They show these years to a partner who must guess the reasons why.

See 11.9 to play tennis with irregular verbs in the past tense.

I enjoyed playing noughts and crosses with irregular forms of the past tense. I split the teams into two groups. One group was noughts and the other crosses. I drew a noughts and crosses board:

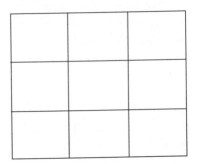

Each team plays noughts and crosses with one student from each team coming up to complete a square. Then I put irregular verbs in, like this:

go	come	think
see	buy	write
sell	catch	read

One student came up, chose a verb and changed it into the past tense. If it was correct, I'd put a nought or cross in the square depending what team they were. The winning team got a full row of Os or Xs first.

The students used to get almost hysterical trying to win a line for their team!

Sue, teaching grammar in Turkey

94

TIMELINES

A timeline can sometimes be a useful way to present a tense or to contrast the meaning of two together. Draw a line representing time on the board and indicate what period of time is referred to in a sentence. Here are some ideas that you can follow or adapt.

I got married last year
NOW

I'll see him next week
NOW

I've lived here for four years
NOW

I was walking along when I met Jim.
NOW

7.6 PAST, PRESENT AND FUTURE
Grammar Focus: All tenses

1 Make a copy of the picture story shown on the next page for each student.

2 Ask students to work out what the story is about and write the story underneath.

3 You can ask students to write the story so it begins with *Yesterday*... if you want them to use past tenses. They start with *Every day*... if you want them to practise using the present simple. Or, to practise using future forms such as *will* or *is going to*... students could start their story with the word *Tomorrow*. Here is a possible version of the story that matches the pictures.

Zelda is a fashion model. Yesterday she got up at ten o'clock. She brushed her teeth and put on her make-up. She had breakfast at eleven o'clock and then drove to the gym to work out. Afterwards she had a drink with her friend Lizzie and they went shopping. Zelda bought a new dress. At five o'clock Zelda telephoned her boyfriend called Jim. They went to the theatre in the evening and then to a nightclub. Zelda went to bed at two a.m.

Follow-on

Ask each student to create their own picture story. When they have finished, they swap stories with their partner, who then tries to write the story out in full.

My favourite classroom activity was when I gave the children sentences on pieces of paper. The children had to put the sentences into three groups. One group was the past, one group the present and one group the future; for example 'I was dead, I am dead, I will be dead.' They laughed a lot and thoroughly enjoyed it and were able to remember most of the rules.

Lottie, a volunteer teacher in India

7.7 STAND IN LINE

Grammar Focus: Comparatives and superlatives

e.g. *He's younger than her, I am the same age as..., I am the oldest.*

1 Ask students to stand up and organise themselves in a line; at one end the youngest and the other end the oldest. This means students will have to ask each other when they were born. Once students are standing in line, ask one of them to compare him/herself with the person standing next to him/her. The people at the ends of the line can use a superlative; e.g. *I am the oldest in the class, I am the youngest.*

2 Now ask the students to organise themselves in different ways; for example by:
- what time they got up (went to bed)
- how long it takes to get to school
- number of brothers and sisters
- number of middle names

Variation

1 Students can run a survey in the class whereby they interview each other using a form they copy from the board like this:

	Piotr	Barbara	Tomas	Macek
Brothers and sisters				
Date of birth				
Number of middle names				

2 They write a summary of the results; for example:
- Piotr has the most brothers and sisters.
- Tomas is the oldest.
- Barbara has the same number of middle names as Macek.

> My worst teaching moment was when I was asked a grammar question that I didn't know the answer to. But after that moment I made sure I knew it...never be afraid to check on something you think you got wrong and come back the next day to re-explain it.
>
> Vicky, on teaching grammar in New Zealand

7.8 THE JOB INTERVIEW

Grammar Focus: *The present perfect* and questions about the past and present e.g. *I've worked in France for three years, Have you ever...*

1 Ask students to write down a job they would like to do in the future or their current job.
2 Students imagine they have a job interview for that job and must write ten questions they would expect to be asked. Help them if necessary by suggesting questions such as:
- *Have you travelled much before?*
- *Have you ever been in charge of people before?*
- *What did you study at school?*
- *Have you had responsibilities in your current job?*
- *What are your strengths?*
- *Why do you want this job?*
3 In pairs they take turns at being the interviewer and the job applicant. They give their job title and questions to their partner who interviews them. The partner can add more questions if they wish.

COMPARING ANSWERS
Before checking answers, sometimes let students compare their answers and discuss why they have answered in a certain way. This allows stronger students to help others and it means a student doesn't necessarily have to lose face in front of the whole class.

7.9 MY ROOM

Grammar Focus: Prepositions of place

e.g. *behind, opposite, in front of, between, next to...*

1 Draw a diagram of a room on the board, like this:

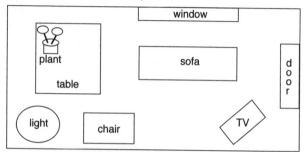

2 Students describe the position of the objects in the room. Help them with any words they need such as *opposite, next to, between* etc.

3 Students draw their own room. In pairs they take it in turns to describe their room. Their partner, without looking, must copy the room on a piece of paper. At the end the students compare their rooms to see how similar they are.

7.10 I AM THE LAW!

Grammar Focus: Modals and verbs for describing rules, obligations and permission

e.g. *must, have to, should, ought to, can*

1 As a class brainstorm ten rules in the students' country. If students come from different countries, then it will be interesting to hear differences. Write each rule on the board using the modal verbs; for example:

- *You have to drive on the right-hand side of the road.*
- *You have to pay taxes to the government.*
- *You can drink alcohol when you are eighteen.*

2 Ask students to work in pairs or groups of three. Imagine they are the government of a new country. They write ten rules for their country.

3 At the end, one student from each government stands up and reads out their rules. When everyone has read their government's rules, the class votes on which country they would most like to live in.

   (Note: if you are teaching in a politically-sensitive region, it might be sensible to make clear this is not a real country – or use a different exercise, for example imagine they are the bosses of a new company or the headteacher of a new school.)

▇▇▇ 7.11 IF I RULED THE WORD

Grammar Focus: First or second conditional

If + present simple —> will ('ll) + verb

If + past simple —> would ('d) + verb

This is a variation on **7.10**. Students follow the same procedure but prepare a list of statements about how they will or would govern a new country using the structures.

For example, in a class where students compete to become president, they might use the first conditional: *If I become President, I'll...*

In a class where they imagine what they would do, students would use the second conditional: *If I became President, I'd....*

> One of my best grammar lessons was teaching the third conditional which is really hard. I asked one student to try to think of an example sentence. He was the Director of the Czech State Radio and described how he lost his wife and got arrested during a pre-Velvet Revolution demonstration. Finally, he said 'If I hadn't run down the side street by the National Theatre, the police wouldn't have caught me.'
>
> Pete, teaching in Prague

▇▇ 7.12 AT THE RESTAURANT

Grammar Focus: Countable and uncountable nouns

e.g. some wine, a glass of wine, some cheese, a plate of pasta, some roast potatoes, a slice of bread

1 Explain to the students that they are at a restaurant. Ask them to suggest dishes and food to put under the headings of a menu. Write their ideas on the board like this:

<u>Starter</u>
Garlic bread
Onion soup

<u>Main Course</u>
Fish and chips
Lasagne

<u>Dessert</u>
Fruit salad
Ice cream

2 When you have plenty of ideas on the menu, write some phrases on the board to use at the restaurant:

   ■ *I'd like some / a plate of / a bowl of*   ■ *Would you like...*   ■ *Do you have any...?*
   Ask some students to give you example sentences combining the phrases and dishes on the menu; e.g. *I'd like some garlic bread, please.*

3 Select certain students to play the part of waiters. If possible, organise the tables as they might be in a restaurant. The rest of the students work in groups of three or four, pretending to be customers in a restaurant. You could ask them to leave the classroom and enter as though they are customers. The waiters can meet them as they come in and place them at a table.

4 The waiters take the orders of the customers who must choose dishes from the menu on the board. Encourage students to ask about the dishes, ask for recommendations or even complain.

> Our Thai-English phrasebook helped with ideas about what type of language to teach. For example, we had the students set up a shop in the classroom to practise phrases for buying and selling food. The only problem was using food we'd never even seen before – we didn't know what it was called in English!
>
> Tom and Judith teaching at a primary school in Thailand

7.13 HOW MUCH WILL YOU GIVE ME FOR THIS EXCELLENT SENTENCE?

This activity can be designed to focus on any grammar point or to revise some you have taught in recent weeks.

1 You need a selection of correct and incorrect sentences based on grammar you have been teaching recently. Fifteen sentences is a good number. (See a ready-made version at the end of this activity.) Write the sentences on pieces of paper or you can simply read them out.

2 Put students into groups of three or four. Tell each group they have £100 to spend at an auction. (If possible, give each team fake money, like the notes in a *Monopoly* board game or make your own.) Define the word 'auction' (*a place where you offer money for something*). Explain that at this auction they can buy a sentence by bidding against other teams. If they think the sentence is correct, they should try to buy it. If it is incorrect, they may still bid in order to trick other teams into buying.

MIXED ABILITY GROUPS
When grouping students, it's useful to put stronger students with others who are finding the language more tricky. That way they can help each other.

3 Read out the first sentence and the teams start bidding. When a team buys one, it is important to note down how much of their £100 they have spent.

4 Auction all the sentences. At the end, tell the class which sentences were correct and see which team bought the most correct sentences. They are the winners. Ask students what is wrong with the incorrect sentences and why.

READY-MADE AUCTION
Here are fifteen sentences which include grammar normally taught at low intermediate level and above which you could use. Eight of them are incorrect. See the explanation of the incorrect sentences afterwards. You may want to give these to your students.

(a) I left school in 1973.
(b) I have begun university in 1975.
(c) How long have you worked here?
(d) Have you ever been in France?
(e) Could I have a cup of tea, please?
(f) Do you have any informations about bus times?
(g) If we leave at 5pm, we'll arrive at 10pm.
(h) You must to drive on the left.
(i) I have longer hair as him.
(j) I'm meeting her at 3 o'clock.
(k) I'll see you last week.
(l) By 2050 people will have landed on Mars.
(m) Everest is biggest mountain in the world.
(n) Look at the clouds. It's going to rain.
(o) I buyed this jumper in the sales.

(a) (c) (e) (g) (j) (l) (n) are correct. The rest are incorrect. Here is why:
(b) The past simple describes a finished action at a specific time. Not the present perfect.
(d) *to France* not *in France*.
(f) *Information* is an uncountable noun so doesn't have a plural -s.
(h) You can't follow a modal verb (*must*) with *to* before the next verb.
(i) *than him* not *as him*.
(k) We're talking about the future not the past. *Next week* not *last week*.
(m) You need the article *the* before a superlative.
(o) *Buy* is an irregular verb. *Bought* not *buyed*.

Chapter 8

Summer Schools and Young Learners

The language summer school is a particular kind of event and needs a particular kind of chapter. In the UK, summer schools are very popular and around the world you'll find that many schools now offer them as an add-on to the normal academic year. Summer is the season for "young learners" to spend a couple of weeks chasing each over big open playing fields, kicking footballs around, getting lost on excursions and outings to historic landmarks and somewhere amongst all this they have some language lessons.

WHAT IS A YOUNG LEARNER?

The term *young learners* refers to anything from five year olds to twelve year olds. However, children and teenagers can vary so much in terms of maturity that you may find teenagers who are still 'childlike' or who are very adult. You'll also find that some of the activities in this chapter will work very well with adults who enjoy learning by doing.

So the requirements for a teacher extend not just to teaching English but being able to arrange a cricket match, direct a theatre production, lead the arts and crafts option; whatever your extra talents, a summer school will bring them out.

What you find in this chapter is a list of ways to get the most out of a summer school, including tips on how to set up sports activities and project work. You'll also still need the activities in other chapters because you'll be teaching the students formally in the mornings. However, dealing with long afternoons of kids with boundless energy is the real focus of this chapter.

Summer school teaching is also about teaching children and teenagers, so if you are teaching these age groups on a regular basis you should find some useful hints and tips.

We were the first falangs [white people] they'd ever seen and after my experience teaching in British schools, Thai kids was so rewarding to teach. They wanted pronunciation help so we chanted the alphabet and named objects round the classroom... I only wished we'd had a photocopiable board game or two.

Tom and Judith in rural Thailand

Sport and games

8.1 THE RED CARD

Team games such as football, cricket, rounders or baseball on a summer school are useful for two particular reasons. Team games allow everyone to be involved and, secondly, they require students to communicate. One way to ensure students communicate in English is to carry a red card (rather like referees use in football matches to indicate a player must be sent off for a foul). If, during a match or competition, you hear any student speaking a language other than English, you show them the red card and they must leave the field for one minute during play. This will quickly make sure everyone uses English rather than let the team down.

8.2 INVENT A SPORT

When you start to run out of sporting ideas for kids to play and even the students can't face yet another football match, ask students to invent a new one.

1 Put students into groups and give each group different sporting equipment. For example, a football, a net, a hockey stick and a rope – whatever you have lying around.
2 Each group has 30 minutes to devise a new sport using only this equipment. Once they have devised the game, they present it to the other teams and teach them how to play.
3 Alternatively to the previous stage, ask each team to write down how their game is played with instructions and rules. When they have finished, they swap their set of rules and equipment with another group and must try to learn to play the other team's new sport.

For less athletic students, for example those who prefer playing chess or Monopoly, ask them to invent a new board game using similar principles.

(Thanks to Pip Stallard who originally described a similar idea.)

8.3 IT'S A KNOCKOUT!

"It's a Knockout!" takes its name from an old TV show where teams competed to finish first over strange and bizarre obstacle courses.

1 Design an obstacle course. Decide how long the track will be and then place a series of obstacles along the way. This will depend essentially on whatever equipment you have lying around the school gymnasium. You could include a hurdle to jump over, hoops to crawl through, a sack to jump over a certain distance in, part of the course where they have to hop on one foot or climb a rope. You will need identical tracks for each team.

2 Divide up the teams at the starting position. One person from each team starts. When they have completed the course, the team member runs back the length of the field to his/her team and the next runner leaves (like a relay race).

3 An additional element is for competitors to carry a bucket of water with them and fill up a container at the end of the course. When one member of a team has completed the course and poured their water into the container, they run with the bucket back to the next member of the team who then sets off with a full bucket. There are two ways to win this version of the competition: as the team who finishes first and as the team who delivers the most water to the end of the course. (Make sure students bring in spare dry clothes on this day!)

(Thanks to Ben McDonald and Tom Welham for this idea.)

> **FIRST AID**
>
> The combination of youthful enthusiasm and physical sporting competition gives the perfect conditions for someone to get injured. If a child is injured while you are in charge, don't panic – it's not your fault, these things happen. On UK summer schools the law demands that someone is appointed to be in charge of First Aid who has been trained in basic First Aid skills. Make sure you know who that person is. Also make sure you know where the First Aid box is kept. If you're abroad and don't speak the language, you need to be certain there is someone who can call for an ambulance or ring the parents in case of emergency.

Excursions

Most summer schools will include some kind of trip or visit to a place of interest. Your main concern on such trips is not to lose anyone! Simply counting the students off the bus and counting the same number back on at the end of the day will constitute success in itself. However, you can also use the day to raise the students' interest in a number of ways and to give them opportunities to use English.

Before taking students on a trip or excursion, use part of a lesson to help them read about the place you are visiting. You'll need some brochures to use in the class. These will be available from the local tourist office or, if you have internet access, download some texts from the net. To show what you can do with the texts, here is an example of some tourist information about the Tower of London, followed by ways to use it in class for language practice.

> **AN INSTANT LESSON**
> See 10.11 for a full-length lesson based around using this text.

THE TOWER OF LONDON

The Tower of London is one of the capital's greatest landmarks. It has been a home and a prison for the Kings and Queens of England. It was built by William the Conqueror in 1078, and today you can see the Queen's priceless Crown Jewels there. There are free guided tours every hour. And don't miss the Bloody Tower from where many never returned. Finish your visit with a boat trip down the Thames River back to the centre of London.

Underground: Tower Hill
Buses: 7, 23, 37, 100, D1, D8
River ferry: Depart every half hour
Suggested time for visit: 2hrs 30 mins.
Adults: £12.00
Children (5-15): £7.80
Family Ticket (2 adults, 2 children): £25.00
Discounts available to groups, school visits, students and OAPs.
Opening Times: Mon-Sat 0900-1700, Sun 1000-1600

▨ ▨ 8.4 INFORMATION GAP

1 Photocopy part of the text. Cover different words or phrases with correction fluid on the two texts to create two different versions, like this:

_____ is one of the capital's greatest landmarks. It has been a home and a prison for the Kings and Queens of England. It was built by _____ in 1078, and today you can see the Queen's _____there. There are free guided tours every hour. And don't miss the Bloody Tower from where many never returned. Finally, take a boat trip down the River Thames back to _____.

The Tower of London is one of the capital's greatest landmarks. It has been a _____ for the Kings and Queens of England. It was built by William the Conqueror in _____, and today you can see the Queen's priceless Crown Jewels there. There are free guided tours _____. And don't miss the Bloody Tower from where many never returned. Finally, take a boat trip down the River Thames back to the centre of London.

°You may photocopy this quiz.

2 The students work in pairs with one student receiving the first text and the other the second text. They have to ask each other questions to get the missing information in their text.

If they have difficulty, help them by providing the necessary questions:
- *What is one of the capital's greatest landmarks?*
- *What has it been for the Kings and Queens of England?*
- *Who built it?*
- *When did he build it?*
- *What can you see in it?*
- *How often are the guided tours?*
- *Where does the boat trip go to?*

For more ideas on helping students understand a text see activities 6.3, 6.4, 6.5 and 10.7.

▪▪▪ 8.5 ABBREVIATIONS

A simple but important task is to have students circle all the abbreviations they can find in the text. Tourist information often contains abbreviations and students can find it difficult to follow. When they have finished, write up the abbreviations they have found on the board and see how many they can guess. (Abbreviations in the Tower of London text are *hrs, mins., OAP, Mon, Sat, Sun.*)

> **ESTABLISH ROUTINES**
> Children like routine as well as lots of variety. So if you have the class all morning or all day, follow a familiar pattern. For example, first thing in the morning sing a song you have learnt together, Next, introduce some new English and practise with some games and activities. Mid morning can be for project work with quiet periods for drawing, cutting, pasting and colouring. At the end of the morning read a story to the group.

▪▪▪ 8.6 AT THE TOURIST OFFICE

In this activity students practise the language they'll need to ask for details such as entrance times and admission fees.

1 Give each student a copy of a text similar to the Tower of London information with details of times, prices and transport details.

2 Students imagine they are at the tourist office and must prepare a list of questions they want to ask; e.g.
   - *What's the nearest underground station to the Tower of London?*
   - *What bus can I catch?*
   - *How long should I spend at the Tower?*
   - *I'm going with a friend. How much will it cost?*
   - *What time does it open on Sundays?*

3 Students take it in turns to play the part of the tourist and the tourist information person. The tourist asks their questions and the information person uses the text to give answers.

   You can extend this activity by bringing in lots of different brochures. Set up different tourist information tables around the room with a student in charge of each table and lots of brochures at each one. The other students walk around asking questions about where to go, what to do, how to get there and the information people must try to find out the answers.

> **PLAY-ACTING**
> Kids are great mimics and up to a certain age are unselfconscious. So lots of game type activities which involve them play-acting will work well.

8.7 RUNNING DICTATION

This activity works with any text but don't choose one that is too long. The descriptive section of the Tower of London text is about right.

1 Divide the class in two. At one end of the classroom the students sit with a pen and paper and their backs to the rest of the room. The other students stand at the other end of the room.

2 On the wall next to the students who are standing place a few copies of the text so that everyone can read it.

3 To each standing student allocate a sitting partner. The standing student must read part of the text, memorise it, run to the other end of the room and dictate it to their sitting partner. The partner writes down what they hear. The running student runs back and tries to remember the next part of the text and so on.

4 The winning pair is the one which finishes first and has a correct version of the text re-written.

This activity is excellent for listening, speaking, reading and writing. It's also a good way to produce more copies of the text if you don't have a photocopier.

8.8 LOST TOURISTS

Providing students with the language they need to ask directions on an excursion is useful as it will help them find where they are going, especially in case they become separated from the group and get lost.

1 Make one copy of the map shown here for each student or a copy of a map of the place you are visiting.

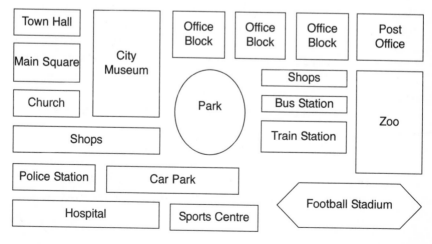

2 Students work in pairs. One student decides where he or she is (e.g. the Main Square) but doesn't tell the other student. The other student is standing at the train station and asks for directions to reach his/her partner. The aim is for the student asking for directions to guess where his/her partner is.

3 Repeat the activity any number of times. You may like to model the activity first by the class having to guess where you are. If necessary, write up useful language on the board such as:

- *Turn right/left*
- *Go past the ..*
- *Go round the...*
- *Cross the road...*
- *I'm opposite / next to / behind / in front of / between....*

REGAINING CONTROL

If you want the students to stop talking or they're making too much noise, clap your hands or tap on the table. You can call out STOP! though this can be hard on the voice and may encourage students to speak louder. Ask all students to look at you. Don't move on to the next stage of your lesson until everyone has stopped what they're doing and is looking at you.

8.9 QUESTIONNAIRES

Once on the trip you can help make the students' experience more interesting by asking them to find answers to some questions.

For example when visiting a museum, prepare a questionnaire for each student, asking them to find out about important dates or people. Giving a prize to the student with the most correct answers will increase motivation.

Another way to devise questionnaires is to gather some brochures about the town you are visiting. Students study the brochures and prepare their own list of questions about the town based on information in the brochures. Then the students swap questionnaires and take these with them on the excursion. Once there, students have to find the answers to the questionnaires without the help of the brochures.

I asked my students to write a questionnaire for foreign tourists. Then we went to Wenceslas Square in the city centre and they talked in English to tourists. It was a great way for them to speak English and put it into practice.

Pete, teaching in Prague

8.10 TREASURE HUNTS

Treasure hunts are similar to questionnaires but they require students to return with some "treasure". Compile a list of items that must be gathered on the excursion. Possible ideas for treasure include:

- a postcard of the town
- a map of the town
- the address of the art gallery
- some water from the fountain in the main square
- a train or bus timetable

Variation

Another type of treasure hunt is one that doesn't involve students finding items or objects but information. For example: *Find out when train X leaves the local station, the name of the shop between the town hall and the pizza restaurant, the telephone number of the local tourist office etc.*

Diaries

Keeping diaries on a summer school is a nice way to have a souvenir of the course and gives the students something to show their parents. Schedule part of the class time every day to writing the diaries. Collect in their diaries but avoid too much error correction. Make it an opportunity for students to express ideas and impressions rather than yet another exercise. If the idea of writing a diary every day sounds a little dull to your young learners, here are three more ways to liven it up.

> See writing activity 9.10 for more on students keeping diaries.

8.11 SCRAPBOOK DIARIES

You can buy scrapbooks very cheaply from a stationer's or students can use blank paper in a file. Students write every day as suggested above, but explain to them that it doesn't have to be just something they write in but can also be a place to stick photographs, postcards, tourist brochures or virtually anything they want to keep.

8.12 WALL COLLAGE
If you have a bare wall in the classroom or an empty notice-board in a corridor, turn it into a collage of the summer school events. Pin up pictures, pieces of writing, photographs and create a colourful tapestry of what students have seen and done in their classes and on their excursions.

> The teachers told students about English traditions and holidays and they had lots of their work displayed on the walls and around the school. They even had a library and their own museum where they showed off all the artistic things that the students had made.
> A language assistant to teachers in Russia

8.13 VIDEO DIARY
With the necessary video equipment you can record different parts of summer school to create a video diary. Perhaps you have a student who could be put in charge of videoing different events. Students could plan and carry out interviews with other students and teachers which they video. At the end of the course hold a video evening for everyone to watch the final diary.

MAKE IT REAL
Younger learners tend to be more interested in what they can do with the language rather than seeing it as an academic subject. So classroom activities should have a relevant end point such as performing a dialogue to the rest of the class or displaying a classroom project on the wall.

Project work
Project work is often scheduled for the afternoons on summer schools and offered as an option. It might range from arts and crafts, drama, a newspaper or a website project. If there aren't projects on offer, then you can run one in your normal lessons.

> My favourite classroom activity with the students was to design a three-day tourist programme stating why foreigners should come to their region and things that they should and shouldn't do. They are really trying to promote tourism in Siberia and some of their parents are looking for ways to make a little extra money so they were keen to tell me about all the things that tourists can do there.
>
> Jane, teaching in Siberia

Projects with younger learners can work well because they draw on the child's interest beyond simply learning English. If a child is interested in music, then that can be incorporated. Projects also encourage more self-responsibility and allow children of different levels of English to work together. All of this leads to self-motivation.

The other side of the coin is to remember that projects go wrong if you haven't thought through all the stages and the language that students need to be pre-taught. Secondly, projects take time and will run over a number of days. They are a huge disappointment if you run out of time and they remain unfinished. So plan it all carefully beforehand and then let the students do the rest.

8.14 NEWSPAPER PROJECT

Building up a class newspaper over a period of weeks is a little like keeping a diary (see 8.11) but with a newspaper, students can research news stories from around the school or include their own features. If you have access to computers, the appearance can be quite professional with lots of copies made. Otherwise, you could produce just one newspaper using a scrapbook or paper stapled together. Here is a series of steps to follow:

1 Brainstorm with the class different parts of the newspaper.
2 Discuss, as a class, what sections students want in their class newspaper.
3 Ask for volunteers to be in charge of different sections of the newspaper. If more than one person, for example, wants to be in charge of the *Sports* section, that's fine because you can create a small editorial team of students to be in charge of *Sports*.
4 Over the next few classes introduce vocabulary which will be useful for students in order to complete the different sections. For example, the *Sports* department will need words to describe winning and losing.

5 Schedule part of every lesson for the groups to meet and work on their part of the paper. Spend time with each group making sure they are on track and providing any language they need in order to write articles. After each meeting one person from every group should tell the rest of the class what their department is doing.

6 Set deadlines for when you want the work to be completed by. You could also arrange a time for other students to come and look at the finished version.

Alternatively, if you think a newspaper is too adult for your learners, then create a classroom comic, where the activities of the school are recorded in picture form with word balloons.

> **My best teaching moment was giving them each a bound copy of their class magazine compiled on the course. They were really happy!**
> Jenny, a teacher and activities leader on a summer school

8.15 CULTURAL RESEARCH PROJECT

If your students are in a new country for their summer school, a useful project is to find out about the culture and habits of the people who live there. Many students will be staying with host families so they are a good source of information. Here is a questionnaire designed for students to use with their host families in the UK. Note that students are expected to think of five more questions of their own to ask in questions 11 to 15.

1. What time do you get up in the morning?

2. What do you normally eat for breakfast?

3. How do you celebrate Christmas?

4. How many holidays do you have a year? (In your own country? Or abroad?)

5. How do you travel to work or school?

6. What is the most popular sport in your country?

7. What kind of a house do you live in?

8. How old are you when you start school in your country?

9. What do you do in your free time at the weekend?

10. What are the most popular types of TV programmes in your country?

11.

12.

13.

14.

15.

MORE SUMMER SCHOOL FUN

Add events to your summer school using the ideas in Chapter 12. To end the course you could hold a talent evening (see 12.3).

Chapter 9

Many teachers make the mistake of leaving writing for "homework" or using it when they run out of things to do (see Chapter 11). It's a mistake because writing for many students is as important as speaking – especially with the rise of email. Writing is also a way to consolidate what students have been taught. It often begins with copying words from the board and, for any student whose first language does not use a Latin-based script or is spoken as it is spelt, English presents peculiar problems.

Writing also needs to be worked on in the classroom because it is not simply spoken language written down. A formal letter has a particular layout, a note left on the fridge will use informal phrases, and a set of instructions needs to be concise and clear. Students may also need help with being creative; their story might need some prompting from you to make the characters more interesting or a descriptive piece could benefit from some interesting vocabulary replacing the adjective *nice* re-occurring ten times in a row.

Remember that writing is for reading and often requires a response. Whenever possible, let students share their written work by exchanging it or pinning it up on the wall awaiting a reply. The key word here is *communication* and you'll find that most of the activities in this chapter seek to achieve just that. They are not designed for students to take home only to hand them to a teacher who then marks them. They are for a communicative classroom with students being as active as they would be in a speaking lesson.

9.1 EMAIL OF COMPLAINT

It is useful to provide students with a model of what you want them to write. On the next page you can see an example of an email complaining about service at a hotel. If you want to teach how to write a letter or email of complaint, make a copy for each student or write it on the board (or even dictate it). Then students underline phrases that they think are useful for complaining. These might be:

Dear Sir/Madam

I am writing to complain about...

First of all...

Second...

Finally...

I am sure that you will understand that this is not acceptable and I expect satisfaction.

Yours faithfully

Using these phrases students can write their own emails of complaint. They could imagine they have been to a bad restaurant, on a terrible holiday or have bought a faulty product. This technique of giving a model first will always help students write well-structured work.

Alternatively, you can provide students with a skeleton of the email as shown below the model on the next page. Students complete the skeleton with their own words.

These techniques will work for many types of text and help to ensure a well-structured piece of writing.

Dear Sir/Madam

I am writing to complain about my recent stay at your hotel. I arrived on the 25th June for two nights. First of all, the hotel receptionist was asleep at the desk and was very slow. Secondly, my room was dirty and the television didn't work. Finally, when I ordered dinner with room service I waited two hours and my food was cold. I complained to the hotel manager who said, "No-one else ever complains".

I am sure that you will understand that this is not acceptable and I expect satisfaction.

Yours faithfully

Dear ....

I am writing to ....

....

....First of all..

....

Secondly, ...

....

Finally, ...

....

....

I am sure that you will understand that this is not acceptable and I

expect satisfaction.

Yours ....

°You may photocopy this page.

MARKING WRITTEN WORK

If you collect written work in to correct and give feedback, check whether the school has a policy on this. Teachers may be expected to give a grade or a mark. Make sure you add comments and praise the work. You can circle errors and ask the students to try to correct themselves. Some teachers use symbols, like these:

☺ (Good work)

☹ (Need to improve)

? (I don't understand what you mean here)

If a student has numerous errors that could result in a returned paper covered in your ink, only correct certain types of error such as the verbs or the punctuation. Hand it back and ask the student to write it out with corrections. Then mark it again focusing on a new problem area. Beware of circling every mistake as the result may be a class full of very dispirited students.

■ ■ 9.2 LETTER CONSEQUENCES

1 Students sit in a circle with a pen and paper. Dictate this opening expression: "Dear Sir or Madam, I am writing to…" Ask students to write this down and complete the sentence with their own words. For example, it could be to complain about something, ask for information, apply for a job and so on.

2 When everyone has finished their sentence, they pass their paper to the right. They read the new letter in front of them and write the next sentence. The letters are passed to the right again and students continue the letters.

3 The activity ends when the student receives their original letter. If a student finishes a letter early, they can start to write a reply letter.

As a follow up students check the letters for errors and re-write them for homework.

Variation

The same activity will also work with a story that begins *Once upon a time…* or you could give a newspaper headline and students create a newspaper article based around the headline.

■ ■ 9.3 EMAIL DIALOGUES

Email English is often like spoken English written down, so sometimes, instead of asking your students to talk about something, ask them to have a dialogue by writing to each other on pieces of paper.

Activity 3.5 provides a series of role-plays for the telephone. Another way to use these role-plays is to carry out the same conversations but using the email dialogue sheet below.

1 Give a copy of the role-play card sheet from activity **3.5** to each student as well as the email dialogue sheet below.

2 Students work through each of the role-plays by writing on the email dialogue sheet and passing it back and forth to a partner. So that everyone is writing at the same time, students play the part of one person, swap email sheets and reply as the other person, unlike the speaking version where they only play one role.

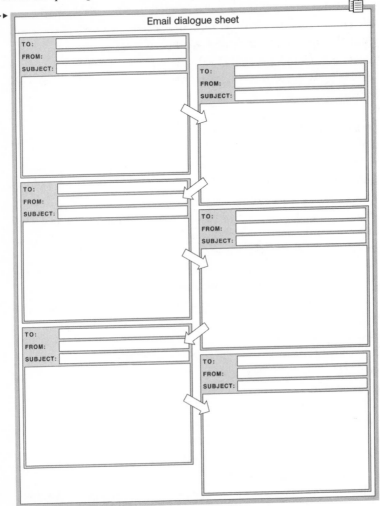

Email dialogue sheet

TO:
FROM:
SUBJECT:

TO:
FROM:
SUBJECT:

TO:
FROM:
SUBJECT:

TO:
FROM:
SUBJECT:

TO:
FROM:
SUBJECT:

TO:
FROM:
SUBJECT:

▨▨▨ 9.4 PAPER PLANES

1 Put students into groups of three. Each group needs a blank A4 piece of paper. With the paper they design a paper plane that must be able to fly. This stage should encourage dialogue in the groups on what the best kind of design might be.

2 When they have finished their creations, ask each group to write instructions on how to create their paper plane. (It would be useful to teach words and phrases like: *fold, in half, across the page, diagonally, from corner to corner.* This can be taught by you holding up a piece of paper and creating your own plane. As you create it, write up the key words and phrases on the board.)

3 When the instructions are complete, one group swaps their instructions with another. The groups must now try to create the plane by following the instructions.

4 Groups see if their planes fly and compare their design with the originals.

▨▨ 9.5 RECIPES

In this activity students receive a recipe in the wrong order and must re-arrange it correctly. Then they study the type of language used in a cooking recipe before writing their own.

1 Make copies for each student of the recipe shown below in which the instructions are in the wrong order. Students may find some of the vocabulary new so it's a good idea to bring in some of the ingredients to class to illustrate the new words. You will need to mime or demonstrate words like *divide, add, knead.*

2 Students decide on the correct order by numbering the steps 1 to 9.

CHEESE AND TOMATO PIZZA

(a) Divide the dough into four balls.

(b) Cover the base with chopped tomatoes and cheese.

(c) Add the yeast, water and sugar to the flour and mix together to make dough.

(d) Mix 25g of flour with a teaspoon of salt.

(e) Leave the dough for two hours. It will double in size.

(f) Mix 15g of yeast with 250 ml of warm water and a little sugar.

(g) Place one ball in a flat pan and spread it out to make the pizza base.

(h) Knead the ball of dough for ten to fifteen minutes.

(i) Bake it in a hot oven for twenty minutes.

°Photocopiable   Answers: 1d; 2f; 3c; 4h; 5e; 6a; 7g; 8b; 9i

3 Students write a recipe of a dish from their own country.

See 12.1 where students cook and present their recipes.

9.6 WRITE A JOB ADVERT

1 Students suggest ways in which you can find a new job. Possible answers might include through a friend or family connection or perhaps by sending your CV out to lots of companies. If no one suggests looking at job adverts, then you will have to suggest it.

2 Bring in some job adverts from newspapers or off the Internet. Spread them round the classroom. Tell students to look at them and make a list of the information included. At the end, ask for their ideas and make a complete list on the board. This might include:

- job title
- salary
- job description
- qualities required
- educational background/qualifications required
- previous work experience required
- information on how to apply
- contact details
- deadline for applications

3 Students think of a job that they would like to apply for and design their own job advert. When they have finished, these can be pinned around the classroom for other students to read.

Follow-on

Students select one of the adverts and write letter of application for it or you could have role-plays where one student is the interviewer and the other student applies. Allow students time to think of the type of questions that might be asked.

Activity 7.8 will work well in a lesson on applying for a job alongside this activity.

Variation

A similar activity can be done with adverts for products. Bring in adverts. Students identify the various contents such as a slogan and details about the product. They then design their own advert for an imaginary product. Alternatively, hand out photos of products and students create an advert for the product.

 9.7 DESCRIBING SOMEONE

Bring in some pictures of people.

1 Students choose one picture and write a description of the person in the picture.
2 The pictures are collected in and put in the middle of a table or on the floor. Students sit around the pictures and take turns to read out their descriptions. The rest of the group listen and guess which person is being described.

With large classes, put the students into groups of six with six pictures in the middle.

> My favourite classroom activity was teaching poetry. In fact my best teaching moment was teaching this poem:
>
> One, two, three, four,
> Please go and open the door,
> Five, six seven, eight,
> Hurry up, you'll be late!
>
> We worked on words that rhymed with 'four' and 'eight' (a great exercise, by the way), then they wrote their own second and fourth lines. One enthusiastic football fan came up with:
>
> One, two, three, four,
> Jim's balls are on the floor,
> Five, six seven, eight,
> Oh look, here comes Kate!
>
> This was also my worst teaching moment!
> Virginia, a volunteer teacher in Tibet

9.8 STORY BUILDING

When you want students to write stories, there are various ways to prompt their imaginations. Here are a few ideas.

- Give students a selection of pictures or cartoons and ask them to discuss how they are connected. (The pictures don't have to be really connected in any way but let students' imaginations do the work.) When they are ready, students can write a story based on their ideas or they could produce a group story with one person being the secretary and everyone suggesting the story.
- Give students the opening sentence to a story such as *The sun was going down over the hills as Ben woke up. It was evening but he had slept all day after a long, long night* and ask them to finish it. Or give them the closing sentence such as *The church bell rang a final time as Sue walked away. She sighed with relief. The nightmare had ended.*
- Play three or four sound effects (sound effect tapes or CDs can be bought cheaply) and students make notes on what they think is happening in each sound. Then they write a story linking the events together. With children, ask them to create a comic strip based on the sounds.
- Place five or six objects on a table and have students include them all in a story. To provide more of a context tell students a crime has been committed and all the objects are connected in some way.
- Once students have written a story, let them read each other's. To develop stories students can read their partner's story and then prepare ten questions about the story which aren't answered in the text; e.g. *What was the colour of the main character's hair? What was the weather like? Where was the woman from?*

They hand the story back to the author who then re-writes the story including information which will answer the questions. This is a good way to get students thinking about their reader and making the stories more interesting and imaginative.

> We were told to teach grammar and nothing else but decided not to as we didn't know any ourselves so we taught poetry, debating, story telling...
> Will, on volunteer teaching in Kenya

Also see 2.10 for story telling or writing

9.9 COMIC STRIPS

Photocopy a cartoon strip either from a newspaper or children's comic and cover the words in the word balloons with correction fluid. Let it dry and make enough photocopies for each student to have one. Students have to write their own speech in the empty speech bubbles. Children will especially enjoy this and will be happy to make their own comic strips.

9.10 DEAR DIARY

Encourage students to start keeping a daily or weekly diary about their lives. You could provide time in class once a week for students to write in their diaries. It's advisable not to correct students' diaries as these are quite personal and the emphasis should be on students simply writing. Also see activities 8.12 and 8.13 for more ideas on writing diaries or journals.

9.11 AGONY AUNTS

1 Draw a picture on the board of someone looking sad with a broken heart.

Ask students "Why is he sad?" Elicit that his girlfriend has left him. Ask students who he can talk to about his problem. Elicit the idea of writing to magazines. These are sometimes called Agony Aunts in English.

2 Students write a letter from this man to an Agony Aunt about his problem.

3 Students swap letters and reply to the letter as the Agony Aunt giving advice to the writer of the letter.

It's helpful to bring in some examples of letters from magazines or provide a model of the type of letter you want students to write (see activity 9.1 on providing models). Alternatively, you could write these useful phrases on the board to help students:

- *Dear Agony Aunt*
- *I writing to tell you about my problems…*
- *Firstly / Secondly / Also*
- *I don't know what to do…*
- *I'd be grateful for your advice…*
- *Yours unhappily…*

See 10.10 for a complete writing lesson based around writing an advertisement to find a partner in the newspaper.

■ ■ ■ 9.12 CORRECT ME IF I'M WRONG

This activity will work with virtually any piece of writing. It's a good way for students to practise speaking and listening but it's also a good activity to focus students on how to write a similar text. All you need is to take a piece of writing and copy it, but put different words in to make an incorrect text. An example for you to photocopy is on the next page.

1 Put students into pairs calling one of them A and one of them B. Give A the correct text and B the incorrect text.

2 Student B reads out the incorrect text. Student A listens. As soon as Student A hears a different word he/she shouts *STOP!* Student B has to guess what the correct word is. Student A can give clues or answer questions but cannot say the actual word. Student B corrects the word and continues. e.g.

B: *Dear Mr Smith*

A: *Stop ! Not Mr but when a woman is married….*

B: *Mrs*

A: *Correct*

3 At the end, ask students to produce a similar piece of writing. With this particular example students could design their own adverts for summer schools. These could be pinned up and chosen by other students who then write a letter for more information.

STUDENT A

Dear Mrs Smith

I'm writing to ask for information about your English language summer school. Please could you send me a brochure. I'm especially interested in the visits to historic towns. I also enjoy playing sport so would like to take part in the football and tennis afternoons. I hope to take my holiday in June so please enclose dates and fees. I look forward to hearing from you.

Best regards

-------------------------------- cut along this line -------------------------------

STUDENT B

Dear Mr Smith

I'm speaking to ask for information about your Spanish language summer university. Please could you email me an advertisement. I'm especially interested in the visits to amusement parks. I also enjoy watching television so would like to take part in the film and quiz evenings. I hope to take my holiday in July so please send dates and prices. I look forward to meeting you.

Best wishes

°You may photocopy this.

Chapter 10

Survival Lesson Plans

If the previous chapters have all been about recipes and serving up activities and exercises, this chapter is about the three course meal – the complete lesson plan. It brings together some of the ideas presented so far and adds a few new ones. Clearly, it's impossible to predict here what lessons you'll be expected to teach or how long your lessons last and how many students you have in them. But you will find series of ideas tied together into a theme that you can edit or add to according to your needs. Just reading through them should also spark off other ideas or ways to adapt them to different language aims. Above all they may be the lessons that get you through your early weeks of teaching. Some of them list a series of activities from this book with tips and hints on how to link them. Other plans offer more extensive notes or new material.

FILING YOUR PLANS
You'll find that many of your lessons can be adapted and re-used with other classes. It's a good idea to get into the habit of safely filing your lesson plan, notes and materials in a ringbinder or folder so they are easy to find next time.

10.1 A FIRST DAY LESSON

1 To learn the names of every one in the class play 1.1.

2 Follow on with activity 1.2 *Variation 2* to find out more about the students.

3 Students suggest questions and interview you. Then they interview a partner (see 1.4).

4 Students write a profile of their partner (1.11) using the information they have found out. Collect in this writing to study the students' ability.

5 If you have any time left at the end, pass some photos round of your family and home and tell students about life in your country (see 1.12). Ask students to work in groups and make a list of differences and similarities between your country and their own.

OVER-PLANNING

As a general rule-of-thumb, always plan for more than the time you have available. After all, you can always use anything left over in the next lesson. If you do run out of things to do before the end of the lesson, see Chapter 11 for more ideas.

10.2 A BEGINNERS' LESSON

It's becoming increasingly impossible to find an absolute beginner in English around the world. You'll find that many students know the word "Hello" and have heard English music or seen an advert written in English. But faced with a first day lesson with total or virtual beginners here's a sixty-minute lesson to follow.

1 If possible have the students sit in a semi-circle with plenty of space to move around.

Wave your hand and say "Hello". Repeat a number of times waving to different students. Gesture to students to reply by waving and saying "Hello" by beckoning with your other hand. Gesture to different students and exchange "Hellos". Encourage students to wave to each other and say "Hello" across the room.

REPEATING

Having students repeat a sentence after you as a class, then individually and then to each other is a good way to introduce new language. Do it again and again. Students can't repeat new language enough at this level. This type of repeating is also sometimes referred to as drilling. Choral drilling when the whole class repeats is a good way for students to build confidence. Individual drilling is a quick way for you to check that each student can say the new language.

2 Point to yourself and say your name. Encourage students to point to themselves and say their names to the class and to each other. Point to yourself and say "My name's ....." Repeat this a number of times. Gesture to a student to say the phrase. Continue round the class until you feel all the students can say "My name's X" confidently.

3 Ask students to stand up by raising your palms upwards. Walk amongst them and wave at them all and say "Hello. My name's ...." Encourage them to walk and do the same, waving and introducing themselves to each other. If there isn't space to let them walk around the room, they can wave from their seats to each other. Direct students to sit back down with your palms pushing down.

4 Draw two faces on the board, like this:

- Point at one and say "What's your name?".
- Point at the other and say "My name's Jack. What's your name?".
- Point back at the other and say "My name's Jill."
- Repeat this sequence. Then, pointing at the faces on the board gesture to the class to repeat after you the three sentences. Repeat this process pointing at different students to repeat the sentences.

5 When you think the class sound fairly confident with the question and answer, point at yourself and say "My name's …." And gesture to a student and say "What's your name?"

IF AT FIRST THEY DON'T SUCCEED…
If one student doesn't reply to you, try another student. If students can't reply to your question or say the new language, then have the whole class repeat the language again. Don't worry. It just means the students need more time to practise before trying it on their own.

6 Gesture from one student to another to say "My name's…" and ask the other student "What's your name?". When everyone has tried saying it, you could ask the students to stand and walk around saying to each other, "Hello, my name's….What's your name?".

7 Now introduce the sentence "Nice to meet you" by shaking the hands of students. When students have all practised saying it, put it with the other sentences to produce the dialogue:

"Hello. My name's…What's your name?"

"My name's…Nice to meet you"

Again, make sure the students repeat the dialogue as a class, individually and by talking to each other.

8 You can conclude by writing up the sentences on the board in word balloons coming from Jack and Jill, like this:

MORE TIPS FOR BEGINNERS' LESSONS

Here's how you might teach some more useful language at this level:

- Introducing numbers – Roll a dice and say the number shown.
- Offering something to drink or eat – take in a can of coke, a bottle of water, bar of chocolate or any well-known item and teach language like:
  Would you like a...?
  Yes, please/No, thank you.
- Members of the family – draw a family tree or show photos of your family. Ask students to do the same.
- Countries and nationalities – take a map of the world and teach
  Where are you from?
  I'm from....(country) I'm ...(nationality)

LEAD-IN

It's a good idea to start a lesson with a lead-in such as brainstorming words or using pictures.

▪ ▪ 10.3 A VOCABULARY LESSON

1 As a quick warmer to the lesson write up the clothes listed in 5.3 with the missing vowels. Ask students to complete all ten words first.

2 Ask students to think of three adjectives for each of the ten items of clothing and write them out in the correct order; e.g. *Large, black, cotton trousers.*

You could write up the rules of order of adjectives shown in 2.8 on the board to help the students.

3 Follow the instruction in activity 9.7 where students write a description of people in pictures. In this case, ask students to focus on describing only the clothes people are wearing.

4 Sit students in a circle and play the clothes guessing game described in 2.11.

▮ 10.4 A GRAMMAR LESSON

1 Draw this on the board:

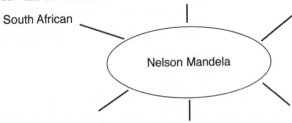

Ask students to work in pairs or groups of three. They have two minutes to list anything they know about Nelson Mandela. An example is given. After two minutes collect in their ideas on the board.

2 Introduce the topic of the past by drawing this timeline of Nelson Mandela on the board.

1918	1952	1990	1993	1994	1999
is born in	*works as*	*leaves*	*wins*	*becomes*	*retires*
South Africa	*a lawyer*	*prison*	*Nobel Prize*	*President*	

Ask students to copy the timeline but to put the verbs into the past simple:

is born = was born works = worked

leaves = left wins = won

becomes = became retires = retired

3 Check their answers and ask:
- Which verbs are regular verbs? (*worked, retired*)
- Which are irregular? (*was, left, won, became*)
- What do we add to regular verbs in the past? (*-ed*)

4 Follow the instructions in activity 7.5 for more practice with the past simple.

5 Complete 7.6 with students telling the picture story in the past and then creating their own.

6 For homework (or instead of using the picture story in **5**) students write a short biography of someone they admire.

10.5 A FUNCTIONS LESSON

1 Begin the lesson with ten minutes of "Hot Topics" (see 3.1).

2 Introduce phrases for discussing using Phrases Poker (3.2) or by designing a board game using the blank board in 3.7. On each square write one of the following:

- *Agree*
- *Disagree*
- *Interrupt*
- *Give an opinion*
- *Ask for an opinion*
- *Suggest a new idea*

Give the students a simple topic to talk about; e.g. *What is the best food in the world?*

When a student lands on a square, they must use a correct phrase to talk about the topic. So, if they land on *Give an opinion,* they might say: *In my opinion Indian food is the most delicious in the world.*

3 Now explain that the students will have more practice with the phrases in **2**. Choose either of the discussion tasks in 3.3 or 3.8.

10.6 A VOCABULARY, GRAMMAR AND FUNCTIONAL LESSON

1 Draw the following on the board:

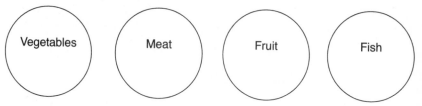

2 In pairs, students write four words in each circle as examples of the type of food given; for example:

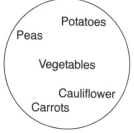

3 Draw two columns on the board and ask students to suggest phrases for the customer and the waiter in a restaurant. Add any others you think might be useful, like this:

CUSTOMER	WAITER
I'd like...	Are you ready to order?
Can I have...?	Would you like...?
What do you recommend?	Can I recommend the...?
Do you have any...?	Do you want ... with that?
Sorry, I didn't order this.	So that's...

4 Follow the procedure outlined in activity 7.12 where students role-play a scene in a restaurant.
5 While students do the restaurant role-play in 7.12, note down any errors you hear and then write them on the board. Ask the class to identify the errors and correct them.
6 Now ask students to imagine they had a bad meal at the restaurant and you want them to email the manager to complain. Follow the procedure in 9.1 and conclude with students writing their emails in class or for homework.

FOLLOW-UP LESSON
You could follow this lesson with activity 9.5 which is about food and recipes.

10.7 A READING LESSON

MORE READING
The steps in this lesson can be used with other articles. You'll also find more ways to use readings in 3.10, 9.1, 9.5, 9.6 and 10.8.

1 Make copies of the article on page 136. Make enough copies to give one copy to a group of three students. Cut the article up paragraph by paragraph, making sure all six paragraphs are kept together (use a paperclip).
2 The original headline of the article was BABY TALK. Write this on the board and ask the class what they think the article might say or be about.

3 Put the class into groups and give each one a set of cut-up paragraphs. The students have to arrange the paragraphs in the correct order. They compare their order with other groups before you give them the correct answer.

4 Ask students in their groups to discuss the two questions in paragraph 1 for a couple of minutes and then discuss the questions as a class.

> **EXTRA EXERCISE**
> You could also use the true/false statements in 6.4 with this reading.

5 Write the following definitions of words on the board and tell the students they will find one corresponding word in the reading.

> a) very old
> b) an animal or plant that died thousands of years ago and is now rock
> c) of the body – the way it works
> d) a, i, e, o, u
> e) what might happen or be true but not a real situation
> f) copy

6 Check their answers to 5 and then ask students to write new sentences using the six words. This is a good way to check they understand them and have learnt how to use them.

7 Put students into pairs and give them ten minutes to prepare seven questions about the reading on a blank sheet of paper. For example, *What century do the words hamburger, skateboard, television and computer come from?*
When they have finished their questions, they swap them with another pair who have to try to answer them.

> **EARLY FINISHERS**
> If students finish early or before others in the class, be prepared to set them an extra task. For example, where students are creating questions for other students in the previous lesson plan, ask them to think of two more.

How do you say the words *hamburger, skateboard, television* and *computer* in your language? For many languages these English words are the same because they are modern twentieth century words. But what about ancient words like *mother*? Why do so many languages have a similar word to *mum, mom* or *mummy*? Scientists in the USA think they may now have discovered the answer.

----------------------------- cut along this line -----------------------------

New research shows that the sounds in these words provide clues to the very first language that humans ever spoke to each other. We can think of these sounds like fossils or the bones of dinosaurs because they tell us about our pre-historic past. They are simple and follow a pattern of consonant-vowel, consonant-vowel; for example, sounds like *na-na, da-da* or *ta-ta*. These are not recognisable words but include sounds we use in our everyday vocabulary.

----------------------------- cut along this line -----------------------------

The scientists studied the speech of babies for their research. This is because babies have no words and only produce sounds when they first make noise with their mouths – what we call *babble*. This babble is the same for all babies of different nationalities. So a German baby will say *da-da* the same as a Japanese baby. This is because babies produce the easiest sounds in a language first: consonant sounds like *dddd* or vowel sounds like *aaaa*.

----------------------------- cut along this line -----------------------------

To find the *original* language, scientists created *protowords*. These are hypothetical words which contain sounds from words in modern languages which are similar. They then compared the sounds and patterns of protowords to the sounds of babies. The sounds were often identical.

----------------------------- cut along this line -----------------------------

John Locke, an expert in infant language and linguistics at Cambridge University, is not surprised that babies' speech or babble is similar. Babies do not have the physiological ability to produce complicated words or adult language so their speech in unaffected and original. He also notes that babies teach their parents sounds and not vice versa. "The first assumption is that infants are imitating adults but it is in fact the opposite. Adults imitate the baby." For example, when a baby says "da-da" for the first time, the father is so happy and repeats "da-da" back again and again, convinced that the baby is trying to say "Daddy". The reality is that the baby finds the sound "da-da" easy to say.

----------------------------- cut along this line -----------------------------

So the first words Adam said to Eve were probably not, "Hello, pleased to meet you, my name's Adam," but possibly, "na na ba ba mmmm mmmm." But for the real answer, ask a baby.

°You may photocopy this page.

▌▌ 10.8 A SPEAKING AND WRITING LESSON

1 For this lesson students will need to use numbers and spelling so review these two areas by using 11.5 for spelling and 5.9 for numbers. You can also play Bingo with numbers. (See 5.7.)

2 Tell the students they have an answer machine on their telephone. They come home one day and find this message. You read out the message and the students make notes:
"Hello, this is Nick Painter. That's P-A-I-N-T-E-R. I'm calling from Travel World about your tickets to Madrid on Sunday 23rd January. I'm afraid there's a problem with the reservation. Can you call me back on 0207 369 8503. Thanks a lot."
   Read it twice if necessary and check that students have the main information.

3 Follow the steps in 3.5 for telephone role-plays.

4 Now repeat the role-plays in 3.5, but this time students communicate by writing as if by email. See 9.3.

▌▌▌ 10.9 A LISTENING LESSON

This is an example of how to adapt a newspaper article into a listening listen. This particular article is full of numbers so is useful for practising what can be a difficult area of language.

1 Draw a picture of a boat on the board.

   Ask students if they have travelled on a similar boat.
   Tell them that this boat is called *The ResidenSea*. Ask them what two English words it combines (*Residence* and *Sea*).

2 Tell students that you are going to read out the article (see page 139) and they must write down every number they hear. (The numbers have been underlined in the text for quick reference.) You will probably have to read it twice.

3 Once students have all the numbers, ask them to listen again and note next to each
number what it refers to. Read the first two sentences as examples:
- *£3.5 million – cost of apartment*
- *£250,000 – cost of service*

3a (Optional stage) You could photocopy the article and students check their answers.
You could also ask them to write questions about the article:
e.g. *How much does an apartment cost?*

4 The article tells us that customers can have an apartment "designed in a special way".
So follow the steps in 7.9 and draw a room on the board, explaining that this is a room
on the ship. Students review prepositions of place and then they draw their own room
on *The ResidenSea* and describe it to their partner.

5 In pairs: one student imagines he/she is a salesman on *The ResidenSea* selling
apartments. The other student is customer with lots of money to spend. The salesman
must explain the main features of the apartment and the customer must prepare
questions to ask. Write the following on the board to help students prepare their ideas:
- *size*
- *number of rooms*
- *design*
- *facilities*
- *cost*
- *service cost*
- *countries the ship will visit*

Students could use their drawings of the apartments in **4** to refer to.

When students are ready they role-play the conversation between the salesman and
the customer.

6 For homework students could write about the apartment for a sales brochure.

An apartment costs £3.5 million. The service costs £250,000 a year. For a businessman from Saudi Arabia this is cheap. He looked at the advertisement for the new home and paid for it after only 15 minutes.

There are 110 similar apartments for sale. The big difference about these apartments, other than the price, is that they are all on a boat that will sail round the world. It will be the first liner ever designed as a permanent home.

The ResidenSea is being built in Norway. It is costing £230 million to build. The boat has 12 decks and every facility you can imagine; hair salons, casinos, tennis courts, a place to practise golf, a theatre, an art gallery, a market and a nightclub.

A typical apartment has 3 bedrooms, 3 bathrooms and a living room of 300 square metres. The owner of an apartment can have it designed in a special way. One customer didn't want a kitchen because she wanted more space for her 300 pairs of shoes. Another customer wanted a bigger space to dance in.

If you have between 2 to 5 million pounds and would like to spend the rest of your life sailing round the world and not paying tax, you must be quick. 80 apartments have been bought. Only 30 apartments are now for sale.

°You may photocopy this. Originally appeared in *The Reporter*, January 2001.

▧ ▧ 10.10 A WRITING LESSON

This is a fun lesson for adult classes and especially good for Valentine's Day. The only preparation is to find some copies of the personal ads from a newspaper or photocopy the ones shown on the next page.

1 Ask the class to suggest ways to find a new partner; e.g. go to a nightclub, through a friend, work. Suggest, "by placing an advertisement in a newspaper" if none of the students do.

2 Give students some examples of personal ads from newspapers to study. Here are some you can copy and use if you don't have access to a newspaper.

43 YR OLD, handsome and looking for partner. Slim, 6'2", affectionate and caring, n/s, likes cooking and gardening.

CUDDLY FULL FIGURED retired 60 year old. Looks for another half to share quiet life. Young at heart.

ROMANTIC GUY, 35, lives in London area, caring, reliable and loving. Good with children and has own business. Seeks beautiful lady for long-lasting friendship.

BLONDE BLUE EYES, 28, wants to meet honest dark and fun-loving n/s. Likes cinema, nightclubs, restaurants. Divorced, two children.

©You may copy this.

3 Here are some tasks to give students to help them with the ads above. Most of them will work with any personal ads:
- ■ Students decide which ads are written by a man looking for a woman and which are from women looking for a man.
- ■ Students circle any words which describe activities; e.g. cooking, gardening, cinema etc. Make a list of these activity words on the board and ask students to suggest more of their own.
- ■ Students underline any adjectives and then decide which adjectives can only describe a man (*handsome*) and a woman (*beautiful*). Can your students think of any more? Make a list on the board.
- ■ These adverts often include abbreviations so check students understand them. Also point out that sometimes abbreviations are used to describe the person, like SWF (single white female).

4 Once students have studied the adverts they write their own. Encourage them to use the words on the board.

5 Pin or blu-tac the finished adverts up on the wall. Students stand and read them all. They choose one to write a letter to. Their letter should describe themselves in more detail and say why they were attracted to the advert.

6 At the end, students can find out who wrote the advert and give them their letter.

By the way, I once did this activity and two students did actually end up going out on a date!

> ## INTEGRATED SKILLS
> This term refers to a lesson where reading, writing, speaking and listening are all combined in one lesson.

■■■ 10.11 AN INTEGRATED SKILLS LESSON

1 Bring in some pictures of different holiday locations. These can be found in holiday brochures. Spread them around the room and ask students to walk around and choose one place that they would like to visit on holiday. If you have more students than pictures, then pair up students and tell them they must discuss and choose a destination together.

2 Students show the class or another student their picture and explain why they chose it.

3 Tell the class they are going to visit London.

4 Organise the class for a running dictation using the Tower of London text. See activity 8.3 and make copies of the text on page 106.

5 After the dictation follow up with activity 8.6 in which students role-play visiting a tourist office. Again, use The Tower of London text for this.

6 Complete the information gap activity in 8.4.

7 Ask students to refer to the picture of the holiday destination they chose at the beginning of the lesson. Tell them to write a similar text about their picture to the one about the Tower of London in 8.4. Remind them that it is for a brochure so they must make people want to visit that destination. If you run out of time, students can finish it for homework.

> ## SET TIME LIMITS
> Telling students "you have five minutes" or "ten minutes" and then counting down "you have one minute left" can help increase their sense of motivation and urgency. Time limits help with activities where students are working on a task in groups or with team efforts such as a running dictation.

Chapter 11

When You Run Out of Things To Do

> My number one tip for any new teacher of English would be to make sure you always have something to hand out like a crossword or quiz to fill 15 minutes if you've run out of things to do.
>
> Julia, teaching in France

Estimating the length of a lesson, especially when it's your first time, can be a real guessing game. You don't know how the students will react to your lesson or how quickly they'll complete a task. You can repeat a lesson many times and the length will still vary. So having a selection of activities up your sleeve to slot in at the end or when your lesson plan finishes early is a real necessity.

11.1 TEST YOUR PARTNER

Tell students to choose five words from the lesson and write a quiz for their partner or another team. The test can be designed using either of these methods:

You sit on a c_____
Or…
It's something you sit on.

11.2 ONE THING I'VE LEARNT TODAY

Students write down one new thing they've learnt today and tell their partner.

11.3 ARE YOU A…?

Imagine you are a famous person. Choose someone; e.g. Nelson Mandela. Your partner must guess who you are by asking you questions. You can only answer *Yes* or *No*.

e.g.

Are you a woman? *No.*
Are you a politician? *Yes.*
Are you popular? *Yes.*

> **FILLERS AND WARMERS**
> The activities in this chapter are called *fillers* because they will slot into virtually any class where you have a spare five minutes. These types of activities are also sometimes called *warmers* as some of them can come at the beginning of the class when you want to "warm everyone up" before the real lesson begins.

11.4 THINK OF A QUESTION

Student A says a new word from the lesson today. Student B has to think of a question that would get this word as an answer.

e.g.

Student A: Chair
Student B: What are you sitting on?

11.5 SPELLING GAMES

Students find spelling in English difficult and even higher levels find a regular review useful (especially with the letters a, e and i). Here are some quick ways to practise:

- Students sit in a circle and one student says "A". The next student says "B", the next say "C" and so on until the group has spelled out the whole alphabet. Now ask them to spell it out backwards: "Z...Y...X..."
- Write a letter on the board (e.g. A) and the words:
  - country
  - food
  - sport/hobby
- Students work in teams and race to think of words beginning with the letter for each of the categories; e.g. Armenia, artichoke, athletics. The first team to get the words wins a point. Then you give another letter.

- Students write out the name of someone famous. They spell the name to their partner but without making a sound. The other student must guess the name by concentrating on the position of the mouth for each letter. This raises awareness of the shape of the mouth for pronunciation.
- Find some international names and/or addresses and students dictate these to each other.

> **REVISION**
> Don't feel you always have to teach something new. Include revision activities in your lessons. Students need time to revise language so make sure that vocabulary is being recycled. These activities will help.

11.6 GUESS THE WORD

1 Sit one student with their back to the board. Write a word from a recent lesson on the board. The other students try to define the word or give clues. The student with his/her back to the board has to guess the word. This game can also be done as a team game with two or more students trying to guess the mystery word first.

11.7 HANGMAN

With hangman, you choose a word and put lines on the board to indicate how many letters are in the word. For example, the word EXCITED would look like this:

— — — — — — —

Students then suggest letters. If they suggest the letter E, you would write it in like this:

E — — — — E —

If they suggest a letter which does not appear in the word, then you draw the first part of a hangman's scaffold. The class have to discover the full word before you draw the entire hanged man.

CULTURAL AWARENESS & SENSITIVITY

Be aware of your students' background. For example, with many learners of English being displaced from their countries due to political unrest, activity 11.7 and the context of hangman may not be appropriate. Similarly, the topic of family is not necessarily the obvious choice for all students escaping from a war. Also, if teaching in a Muslim country, do not refer to alcohol or use newspaper articles about alcohol. In other words, take nothing for granted.

11.8 ON-THE-SPOT CALLS

Ask students to think of the last phone call they made in their own language. Then they tell their partner about the call, describing what it was about and giving details about the receiver. Finally, the two students role-play the call in English.

(Thanks to John Anderson for this idea.)

11.9 TENNIS

Students work in pairs and sit opposite each other. One player goes first or "serves" and says a word. The other player has to say a word that rhymes. The first player has to think of another word that rhymes and so on. When a player cannot think of a word, the other player wins a point. The player then thinks of another word and starts again. The students use tennis scoring to decide who wins. You can also play this game using irregular verbs by using the pattern of infinitive, past tense, past participle. For example:

- Student A (serves): go
- Student B (returns): went
- Student A (returns): gone
- Student B (returns): buy
- Student A (returns): buyed

In this example Student A has made a mistake so the score is *love-fifteen*. If your students don't know how to score in tennis, tell them the first to get ten points is the winner.

11.10 GIVING YOU FEEDBACK

Asking students for feedback on your lessons (after about twenty hours of teaching) is a good way to ensure you are providing them with what they want and you can anticipate problems before they escalate. You may even find out just what a great teacher you really are!

1 Write the following on the board:
   - One thing you like about the lessons
   - One thing you don't like
   - One thing you want more of
   - One thing you want less of
2 Ask students to respond to the above on a piece of paper. They don't have to put their names but explain that you really want them to be honest.
3 Allow about 10 minutes and collect in their papers. Don't mark the English!

11.11 END OF LESSON QUIZ
Quizzes are a fun way to end a lesson. Create teams who have to compete against each other to add to the motivation.

> See activity 12.4 for an instant quiz.

Quizzes can be written for general knowledge or also as a language review. For example, for a grammar quiz the teacher might ask:

- What tense is in this sentence? How long have you lived here? (Answer: The present perfect).
- What's the comparative form of good? (Answer: better)

Chapter 12

Evening Fun and End of Course Events

Many language schools offer extra events for students in the evenings to help with their English or organise parties to celebrate the end of a course. Here are some ideas you can use on your course. You could even suggest these events to your school or incorporate them into your lessons.

12.1 INTERNATIONAL EVENING

If you have students from different countries, invite them to prepare a dish that is typical of their home country. Your role is to lay out a room with some long tables covered in table cloths, paper napkins, plates, knives, forks and spoons and supply some card. Students bring their dishes to the evening, place them on the tables and write the name of the dish on the card. They could add a short description or the actual recipe. When everyone has arrived, students give a short presentation about their dish to everyone gathered. This might include talking about:

- what the dish contains.
- with what other food or drink it is normally served.
- if it is eaten at a particular time of day or time of year.

After the final presentation everyone starts eating!

VARIATION

If all your students come from the same country, ask them to research dishes in other countries and try making them.

12.2 KARAOKE EVENING

A karaoke evening will be familiar to most of your students especially those from Japan, which is the country where it originated. Essentially, karaoke is about someone willing to stand up in front of everyone else and sing along to a song. Play-acting is encouraged, with performers rated on the ability to emulate the original singer.

From a learning point of view, singing along to songs is a great way to improve English so a karaoke evening is a good way to round off a course. It will also combine well with a disco. If you have a budget, many hired professional discos will include karaoke as a featured event. Alternatively karaoke tapes can be bought quite cheaply from music shops. You could even use some lesson time to help students practise the songs and learn the words.

12.3 TALENT EVENING

A talent evening is a way for students to perform in front of everyone else. Here is a list of possible items to include on any talent evening programme:

- a song or a dance from a student's own country
- a performance of a play that students have been rehearsing
- presentation of a video diary (see 8.13)
- poetry readings of work done in class
- an exhibition of arts and crafts done by students or wall collages (see 8.12)

12.4 PUB QUIZ

A pub quiz is a common event in the UK with people creating teams to answer a series of questions on a variety of topics while having a drink. However, a quiz without the drink will also prove popular with students – the number of quiz shows on TV illustrates this.

For a quiz in its simplest form, divide the students into teams. Prepare a list of questions. Read them out and the teams write the answers. At the end, the teams swap answer papers. You read out the answers and the teams mark each other's. Make sure you have a prize for the winning team.

When designing your questions, consider the age, cultural background and interests of your group. Don't assume everyone knows about the latest pop song in your country or that everyone knows (or cares) what the name of Britain's Prime Minister is. Try to make some questions easy and some more difficult.

On the next page you'll find twenty-five questions you could use for the quiz. It's unlikely that all will be suitable for your particular group, but the questions here attempt to be fairly *international* so at least everyone will know some but not all.

Quizzes will also work well in your lessons. If you hold regular quizzes, you can make it the job of the winning team to prepare the questions for the next one.

QUIZ QUESTIONS
Sport
1 What sport uses a puck?
2 What sport is played at the Superbowl?
3 Which two countries hosted the World Cup at the same time?
4 How many pieces does one player have in a game of chess?
5 What three sports are included in a triathlon?

Music
6 What is the last line to the chorus of this Beatles song:
   "All you need is love, All you need is love, All you need is love, love _____ ".
7 What was Elvis Presley's middle name?
   (a) Aaron (b) Junior (c) He didn't have a middle name.
8 Abba won the Eurovision song contest with what song?
9 What dance also means *sauce* in Spanish?
10 What long wooden instrument do Aborigines play?

Geography, science and history
11 What is the longest river in the world?
12 When did Mount Vesuvius destroy Pompeii? In
   (a) 79 A.D. (b) 79 B.C. (c) 97 A.D.
13 Burma, Laos, Malaysia and Cambodia surround which country?
14 Which member of the British Royal Family died in 1997?
15 What country is considered the 'cradle of civilisation'?

Art, literature and film
16 The film capital of America is Hollywood. What is the film capital of India?
17 What does the wizard Harry Potter have on his forehead?
   (a) a spot (b) a scar (c) a plaster
18 Which artist painted *Guernica*?
19 Which spy did the author Ian Fleming create?
20 Complete this line from Shakespeare: "To be or....".

General

21 Which animal is not a mammal? A kangaroo, alligator, cow or tiger?

22 In American English it's called an *elevator*. What is it in British English?

23 What does the '*e*' mean in e-mail?

24 How many people sit on a *tandem*?

25 What type of fruit are Golden Delicious, Granny Smiths and Gala?

ANSWERS

1 Ice hockey, 2 American football, 3 South Korea and Japan, 4 Sixteen
5 Cycling, running and swimming, 6 Love is all you need, 7 (a) Aaron,
8 Waterloo, 9 Salsa, 10 Didgeridoo, 11 River Nile, 12 (a) 79 A.D.,
13 Thailand, 14 Diana, Princess of Wales, 15 Iraq (Mesopotamia), 16 Bollywood
17 (b) a scar, 18 Picasso, 19 James Bond, 20 not to be, that is the question, 21 alligator,
  22 A lift, 23 electronic, 24 Two, 25 Apple

 12.5 SEASONAL EVENTS

One way to introduce customs and seasonal events to students is to celebrate them. At Christmas teach your students carols in English and have a carol evening. At Halloween students hold a costume party. For Valentine's Day make cards. If you're from Britain, tell your students about Bonfire Night – better still let off some fireworks! Ask your students about similar events and special customs in their country. Maybe the whole class or school can celebrate it.

Chapter 13

This final chapter covers some practical matters such as acronyms, useful contacts for job hunting and websites with more teaching ideas. You'll also find questions you may want to find the answers to before taking a job.

Acronyms

There are numerous acronyms in TEFL. Here are a few of the ones you might need at the beginning.

ARELS – Association of Recognised English Language Schools in the UK

CALL – Computer Assisted Language Learning

CELTA – Certificate in English Language Teaching to Adults. This is a trade name TEFL certificate course developed in the UK by University of Cambridge ESOL (UCLES) and RSA

Cert. TESOL – Certificate in TESOL. The certificate course developed in the UK by Trinity College London

DOS – Director of Studies

EAP – English for Academic Purposes – the study or teaching of English with specific reference to an academic (usually a university- or college-based) course

EFL – English as a Foreign Language – English language programmes in countries where English is not the common or official language

ELT – English Language Teaching or Training – a term coined in the UK and designed to replace EFL. It is in use around the world but has yet to catch on in the USA

EOP – English for Occupational Purposes

ESL – English as a Second Language – English language programmes in countries where English is the dominant or official language. Programmes designed for non-English-speaking immigrants in the USA are ESL programmes

ESOL – English to Speakers of Other Languages – a term often used to describe elementary and secondary English language programmes. It is sometimes used to distinguish ESL classes within adult basic education programmes

ESP – English for Specific Purposes – a term that refers to teaching or studying English for a particular career (like law or medicine) or for business in general

JET – Japanese Exchange and Teaching Programme

L1 – First language

L2 – Second language

TYPES OF TRAINING COURSES BEFORE YOU GO

Introductory courses are designed for prospective teachers who want to experience teaching before making the decision to train formally and obtain qualifications. The courses usually last from a week up to four weeks. These are not certificate courses and you will not normally be regarded as a qualified teacher after completion of your introductory course. You will, however, be able to say that you have had some experience of English language teaching. Some schools require trainee teachers to take an introductory course before starting a certificate course.

Certificate courses

The majority of trainee teachers who would like to teach take a certificate course in teaching EFL/ESL. A certificate course provides basic grounding in teaching, lesson development, managing students and, in particular, the different stages of teaching English. Certificate courses are great for trainee teachers who have no experience of teaching – they perhaps have a degree or experience in a totally different field – and want to ensure that they are well prepared for their first 'real' class (as a trainee teacher, part of your certificate course will be to experience practical teaching in a classroom).

Most certificate courses are intensive and run over a four- or six- week period. You can take distance-study courses or take a certificate course on a part-time basis over several months.

Once you have a certificate in teaching English, you can start to apply for jobs at schools around the world. Although there is no single qualification, there are two main certificate courses: University of Cambridge ESOL CELTA and Trinity College London Cert.TESOL. Both are well respected and recognised around the world.

Aside from these two main certificate qualifications, Pitman/City&Guilds have a certificate and many school, colleges and universities have their own certificate course developed in-house. Make sure that you ask the course provider about their qualification and if they will provide assistance in finding a job once you have completed your course.

As well as the basic certificate course, you can also study for additional modules that will gain you experience and qualifications in specialist subjects; for example, teaching young learners or teaching business English.

University of Cambridge ESOL Examinations

University of Cambridge ESOL Examinations
1 Hills Road
Cambridge, CB1 2EU, UK
Tel: + 44 1223 553355
Fax: +44 1223 460278
Email: esolhelpdesk@ucles.org.uk
Website: www.cambridgeESOL.org.uk

CELTA

The Cambridge CELTA (Certificate in English Language Teaching to Adults) is the longest established qualification for English language teachers and has over 8,000 student-teacher enrolments per year. It was developed by the University of Cambridge ESOL. Examinations are managed around the world by the University of Cambridge Local Examination Syndicate.

The CELTA is a pre-experience course, usually run on a four-week intensive basis, though some schools do run part-time courses. CELTA is run in over 50 countries around the world and is taken by more than 10,000 candidates annually. The exam is externally validated by University of Cambridge ESOL; a course normally costs £700-1000 ($1400-2000).

A CELTA course is normally a four-week intensive programme, with an examination at the end (the fee for the examination is normally included as part of the course fee). There are a few part-time CELTA courses, but these are very much the exception. Successful candidates are awarded a Pass, a Pass B or a Pass A.

CELTA courses are, like the Trinity College London Certificate course (see next page), based on practical teaching – with observed teaching practice integral to any course. Pass rates are generally high, since applicants are carefully selected: when applying, you will be interviewed and might have to take a language awareness test.

The CELTA is an initial course which is mostly taken by people with no previous TESOL experience (although some experienced ESOL teachers who have no formal qualifications take this exam to validate their teaching). Although a certain level of academic achievement is recommended by the administrators, there are no specific entry requirements and this is at the discretion of the course provider.

Trinity College London

Trinity College London
89 Albert Embankment
London , SE1 7TP, UK
Tel: +44 (0)20 7820 6100
Fax: +44 (0)20 7820 6161
Email: tesol@trinitycollege.co.uk
Website: www.trinitycollege.co.uk

Certificate in TESOL

The Certificate in TESOL (Teaching English to Speakers of Other Languages) – often referred to as Cert.TESOL is administered by Trinity College London. It has over 4,000 student-teachers enrolments per year and is, like the CELTA (above) a well-recognised Certificate in practical ELT teaching. Trainees are expected to take courses in a foreign language in order to understand the difficulties in teaching a foreign language. No two courses are the same, as course designers can introduce their own ideas and elements, so you will need to verify the details of the specific course. Cert.TESOL courses are usually full-time, intensive and last between four and six weeks, although part-time courses are available at a few centres. The costs are very similar to a CELTA, £700-1000 ($1400-2000).

Pitman/City & Guilds ACE

City & Guilds
1 Giltspur Street, London, EC1A 9DD, UK
Tel: 020 7294 2800
Fax: 020 7294 2400
Email: enquiry@city-and-guilds.co.uk
Website: www.city-and-guilds.co.uk

The Access Certificate in English language teaching (ACE) is a Pitman/City & Guilds qualification developed with Manchester University in the UK. It offers an initial-level certificate for people who have never taught before, for teachers with some experience who want a formal qualification or for teachers experienced in teaching another subject who want to switch to teaching English. The training is in two parts, covering theory and practical teaching activities.

Private Language School Certificates

Some chains of private language schools offer their own 'in-house' training courses and certificates. As a general rule, if these are free and likely to lead to employment or promotion within the organisation, they may be well worth considering. If, however, fees are payable, it is not really advisable to accept any, often vague, assurances that the certificate is internationally-known or respected or that it is equivalent to a CELTA or Cert.TESOL.

Ask to see a list of employers who accept the qualification and contact them to ask if they really do consider this to be a full equivalent of an independent, mainstream certificate.

The best private language school TESOL courses leading to in-house certificates tend to be offered as a supplement to mainstream qualifications (for example, a refresher course) rather than as an alternative.

University Certificate Courses

University Certificate courses are usually short courses running from one to six months and are an alternative to the Cambridge or Trinity certificates (above). These are the most common pre-experience courses available, with almost every university and college in the UK offering some form of English language teaching course. There are also 'in-service' certificate courses available for those teachers who have classroom experience but no formal qualifications.

Distance Learning Courses

Some training courses in English language teaching are offered on a distance basis, though these are not generally popular with employers unless they include an observed period of teaching practice and are externally validated. But if you are already teaching English abroad, they can be a viable option.

Certificates for Teaching English for Business

There are a number of different examinations for teachers who would like to train to teach English for business: for example, Chauncey group, LCCIEB, and Pitman all offer specialist qualifications.

DO I NEED A DEGREE?

In some countries, such as Japan and Korea, a university degree is a legal requirement. In Spain some schools look for teachers to have a degree because government contracts demand it.

Finding a job

The fastest way to find a job these days is via the Internet. Here are some sites that will help your job search:

Good Places to Start

British Council Vacancies
www.britishcouncil.org/vacancies/
   indexmain.html

Edunet
www.edunet.com

International House Recruitment
   Services
www.ihworld.com/recruitment/
   index.asp

Peace Corps
www.peacecorps.gov

Saxoncourt
www.saxoncourt.com

TEFL.com
www.tefl.com

The Times Educational Supplement
www.tesjobs.co.uk/homepage.asp

VSO (Voluntary Service Overseas)
www.vso.org.uk/volunteering/
   education_tefl.htm

ELT-Specific Job Sites:

All English Job
www.allenglishjob.com

Canadian Institute for Teaching
   Overseas (CITO)
www.nsis.com/~cito/CITO.html

Dave's ESL Café: Job centre
www.eslcafe.com/jobs/

Easter School Agency
www.easterschool.com

Edufind ELT Job Centre
www.jobs.edufind.com

EFLTeachingJobs.com
www.eflteachingjobs.com

English Club ESL Jobs Centre
http://jobs.englishclub.com

English Job Maze
www.englishjobmaze.com

English Teacher Recruitment: Greece
www.teach.english.freeservers.com

English Worldwide – Recruitment &
   Training
www.englishworldwide.com

English-International.com
www.english-international.com

ESL Career.com
www.eslcareer.com

ESLclassifieds.com
www.eslclassifieds.com/
   esljobsoffered.html

ESL Employment
www.eslemployment.com

ESL Job Search
www.esljobsearch.com

ESL Resume Database
my.globalesl.net/

ESL Teachers Club
www.eslteachersclub.com

ESL WideWord Teach English
www.eslwideworld.com

ESLworldwide.com
www.ESLworldwide.com

ETNI – Advertising Teaching
   Positions in Israel
www.etni.org.il/anntchadver.htm

Foreignteacher.com
www.foreignteacher.com/
  currentjobs.htm

Global ESL Network
www.globalesl.net

Jobs Offered
www.englishclub.net/
  cgi-bin/jobs/jobs_o.pl

Russian School Placement
www.sv-agency.udm.ru/svfiles/
  school.htm

Saxoncourt & English Worldwide
www.saxoncourt.com

TeachAbroad.com
www.teachabroad.com

Teaching ESL at Kuwait University
www.iteslj.org/Articles/Martin-Kuwait

TEFL Jobs
www.tefljobs.net

TEFLnet
www.tefl.net/jobs/

TEFL Professional Network
www.tefl.com

University EFL/ESL Positions
www.ultimateenglish.com

Work Abroad ESL.com
www.workabroadesl.com

TURNING UP

If you're already in the country or you're intending to travel in a particular country, then turning up at a language school and asking to meet the DOS (Director of Studies) or Manager (often also the owner in small schools) is an effective way of finding a job. You might be lucky and pick up a few hours teaching straight away. Schools like employing people this way because they can meet you and you're already in the country. Make sure you have an up-to-date CV with you and dress up a bit.

HOW MANY HOURS DO I TEACH A WEEK?

Your contract should indicate how many hours you'll teach a week. A reasonable workload is 20-25 hours a week though plenty of teachers do more. This may seem reasonable but remember that this figure represents the actual time in the classroom. It doesn't include the time you'll need to plan, mark work, meet students for tutorials or fill in the paperwork. In some countries a contact hour is not actually an hour. For example, in Poland a contact hour can mean 45 minutes. In Italy it can be 50-55 minutes. So if your contract says you teach 30 hours a week, it may mean around 24 hours in real time.

Recruitment Agencies

There are plenty of commercial recruitment agencies specialising in the English language market – working for a school to help find teachers or helping a teacher find a job. The agencies are normally paid by the employer (the school), though make sure that you check before you sign up! Agencies normally cover a particular region or country – and will help you put together a good CV, send you new job opportunities and even give advice on relocating, accommodation and visas.

Almost all the jobs for ELT or ESL teachers are with English language schools, though there is a small but constant demand within large companies for in-house teachers. The majority of all schools are run on an individual basis, with the director of studies also the person who interviews and appoints new teachers. But there are some major chains of schools which have their own internal recruitment agencies who can help you find a job within the schools in their group. Once you have a job in the group, the internal job-agency often works to help find a job in another school within the group or in a different country.

The biggest ELT employer in the world is the British Council, which has its own recruitment service.

Try these commercial agencies and major international school groups (all in the UK unless otherwise indicated):

Anglo Pacific
Suite 32, Nevilles Court, Dollis Hill
Lane, London NW2 6HG
Tel: +44 (0)20 8452 7836
Agency that specializes in
recruitment in southeast Asia

Avalon House
8 Denmark Street, London
WC2H 8LS
Tel: +44 (0)20 7279 1998
Email: info@avalonschool.co.uk
Web: www.avalonschool.co.uk
Recruitment for its schools in China,
France, Spain, Poland, UK

Bell Educational Trust
Overseas Department, Hillscross,
Red Cross Lane, Cambridge,
CB2 2QX
Tel: +44 (0)1223 246644
Fax: +44 (0)1223 414080
Email: info.overseas@bell-
schools.ac.uk
Web: www.bell-schools.ac.uk
Major group that has schools around
the world; most schools recruit
locally, but this office can provide
contact information

Benedict Schools

3 Place Chauderon, PO Box 270,
1000 Lausanne 9, Switzerland
Tel: +21 323 6655
Fax: +21 323 6777
Email: info@benedict-schools.com
Web: www.benedict-schools.com
Major group with over 80 schools (in
Europe, Africa and America); most
schools recruit locally, but this office
can provide contact information

Berlitz

Lincoln House, 296-302 High
Holborn, London WC1V 7JH
Tel: +44 (0)20 7915 0909
Fax: +44 (0)20 7915 0222
Web: www.berlitz.com
Major group that has over 400
centres around the world; teachers
are trained in the Berlitz way of
teaching

Billington Recruitment

1 Mariners Close, St James Court,
Victoria Dock, Kingston upon Hull,
HU9 1QE
Email: bill1312@hotmail.com
Agency that covers Europe

British Council

Education and Training Group,
10 Spring Gardens, London
SW1A 2BN
Tel: +44 (0)20 7389 4596
Fax: +44 (0)20 7389 4594
Email: assistants@britishcouncil.org
Web: www.languageassistant.co.uk

Provides language assistants to
schools around the world. (See
section on British Council on next
page)

CG Associates

83 Clarence Mews, London
Tel: +44 (0)7802 211542
Email: info@christopherg.co.uk
Agency offering worldwide
coverage.

CIEE

52 Poland Street, London W1F 7AB
Tel: +44 (0)20 7478 2020
Fax: +44 (0)20 7734 7322
Web: www.councilexchanges.org.uk
Looks after the JET (Japan Exchange
Teaching) programme as well as
Teach in China and Teach in Thailand
programmes

EF – English First

Teacher Recruitment, 36-38 St
Aubyns, Hove, East Sussex,
BN3 2TD
Tel: +44 (0)1273 201431
Fax: +44 (0)1273 746742
Email:
recruitment.uk@englishfirst.com
Web: www.englishfirst.com
Major group that recruits for its
schools around the world

ELS Language Centers

400 Alexander Park, Princeton,
NJ 08540, USA
Tel: +1 609 750 3512

Fax: +1 609 750 3596
Email: info@els.com
Web: www.els.com
Major group that works with Berlitz for its language centers – however its 40-plus schools still recruit through this central address

ERC Recruitment
New Tyning, Stone Allerton, Axbridge, BS26 2NJ
Tel: +44 (0)1934 713892
Email: info@erc-recruitment.co.uk
Web: www.erc-recruitment.co.uk
Agency offering worldwide coverage

GEOS English Academy
Compton Park, Compton Park Road, Eastbourne, BN21 1EH
Email: info@geos.com
Web: www.geos.com
Major group that has over 500 schools around the world

GTCE
52 Loampit Hill, Lewisham, London SE13 7SW
Tel: +44 (0)20 8691 6569
Email: info@gtce.co.uk
Web: www.gtce.co.uk
Agency that concentrates on China

International House
106 Piccadilly, London W1V 7NL
Tel: +44 (0)20 7518 6970
Fax: +44 (0)20 7518 6971
Email: hr@ihlondon.co.uk
Web: www.ihworld.com

Major group that has over 120 schools around the world

Linguarama
Personnel Department, 89 High Street, Alton, Hampshire, GU34 1LG
Tel: +44 (0)1420 80899
Fax: +44 (0)1420 80856
Email: personnel@linguarama.com
Web: www.linguarama.com
Major group that has schools around the world

Protocol Professional
Tel: +44 (0)115 911 1177
Email: recruitment@protocol-professional.co.uk
Web: www.protocol-professional.co.uk
Agency that specializes on the UK

Saxoncourt
124 New Bond Street, London W1S 1DX
Tel: +44 (0)20 7491 1911
Fax: +44 (0)20 7493 3657
Email: recruit@saxoncourt.com
Web: www.saxoncourt.com
Major group of schools and recruitment centre that places over 500 teachers per year around the world

Sterling Recruitment
49 Sudbury Ave, Wembley, Middx, HA0 3AN
Tel: +44 (0)20 8903 4424

Fax: +44 (0)20 8903 3566
Recruitment Agency for jobs in
London

Wall Street Institute
Paca de Catalunya 9, 4th Floor,
08002 Barcelona, Spain

Tel: +93 306 33 00
Fax: +93 302 08 29
Web: www.wallstreetinstitute.com
Major chain of over 400 schools
around the world.

WHAT ABOUT OTHER EXPENSES?

Relocation

If you apply for a job from your own country, you'll want to know if the employer is going to pay for your flight. With so many cheap flights round Europe nowadays many employers argue that it's cheaper to travel from London to Barcelona than it is from London to Edinburgh. However, many schools will still pay some kind of relocation fee. This might come at the beginning or end of a contract.

Work permits/visas

For countries where you need a work permit or visa you probably can't avoid travelling to the Embassy. It's a good test of a reputable school if they instantly tell you the process for applying for a permit or visa and know how to organise the paperwork. It's normal for the employer to pay any costs for the permit.

Travel costs

If you have to travel to teach at another site, for example to teach at a company, check whether you will have extra travel expenses. Some schools will reimburse these costs as well as pay you for the time spent travelling.

Accommodation

Schools will often help you find accommodation or find a place to stay for the first few weeks of your contract. Make sure you have some extra money to cover the cost of accommodation at the beginning. Some contracts include rent in the salary and will provide an apartment.

UK Summer Schools

The UK has a very strong summer-school industry (with several hundred schools working the season) that always has a need for qualified teachers. The summer schools cater for students who want to learn English over a summer holiday; these students can be either young learners or young adults.

The rates of pay for work in summer schools is often higher than usual. In the past, some summer schools have not offered very good quality teaching, but with the work of industry associations, particularly the newly-formed EnglishUK (formed from ARELS (Association of Recognised English Language Schools) and BASELT (British Association of State English Language Teaching)) and the British Council (www.britishcouncil.org), the schools are being accredited and standards are now high. Within EnglishUK, the original ARELS department represents private accredited English language schools in the UK and the original BASELT department represents accredited English language schools in universities and colleges.

With so many schools on their lists, it's impossible to fit all these into this book: the best way to search for a suitable school to approach for a job is to use a site such as English in Britain (www.EnglishInBritain.com) or the individual parts of EnglishUK (ARELS or BASELT) websites – all have search features.

English UK
56 Buckingham Gate, London SW1E 6AG
Tel: 020 7802 9200
www.arels.org.uk

British Council
Bridgewater House, 58 Whitworth Street, Manchester M1 6BB
Tel: 0161 957 7755
www.britishcouncil.org

BASELT
University of Gloucester,
Cornerways, Park Campus,
Cheltenham, Glos. GL50 2QF
www.baselt.org.uk

WHAT KIND OF SUPPORT SHOULD I EXPECT?

On arrival, some schools will run inductions for new teachers in which you find out about how the school works – it's a good chance to meet other teachers. They might also provide a few survival lessons in the local language – if they don't, they should be able to suggest someone who can. At the interview stage it's also worth asking what kind of resources the school has, such as textbooks, photocopier, video and so on. A sign of a good school is also one that provides on-going training workshops for teachers with new classroom ideas. In some countries there are teachers' associations which hold conferences and workshops. Some schools will finance staff to attend these.

Volunteer Programmes

The following organisations arrange for volunteer teachers to travel and teach in volunteer programmes around the world, particularly in China and Africa. There are also volunteer groups providing support and teachers in local communities, for example, in regions of the USA where there is a great need for volunteer teachers. The volunteer groups should help arrange your travel, training, accommodation and any visas.

AmeriCorps

www.americorps.org

AmeriCorps is a United States-based organization. The domestic Peace Corps has more than 40,000 Americans in intensive, results-driven service each year. AmeriCorps has built its foundation on teaching children to read, attempting to make neighbourhoods safer, building affordable homes, and responding to natural disasters. AmeriCorps serves with projects such as Habitat for Humanity, the American Red Cross, and Boys and Girls Clubs. After a term of service, AmeriCorps members receive education awards to help finance college tuition or pay back student loans.

AmeriSpan Unlimited

www.amerispan.com

AmeriSpan has become a major force for anyone wanting to study language abroad in Latin America. AmeriSpan's network offers language programmes in nearly every Spanish-speaking country in the Americas.

Amity Institute

www.amity.org

Amity Institute was founded in 1962. It is a non-profit educational exchange programme that gives young people around the world the opportunity to represent their countries, by sharing their languages and cultures in language classrooms of all levels. Amity tries to encourage and enhance international understanding and friendship through the study of world languages and cultures.

Christians Abroad

www.cabroad.org.uk

Provides advice and information for volunteers of any faith who are considering working abroad as a volunteer. It provides job vacancies through a monthly listing newsletter – the majority of its postings are to Asia and Africa. Also visit www.wse.org.uk for online information packs.

Colorado China Council

www.asiacouncil.org

The primary focus of CCC is to send people to teach English, as well as other academic subjects, at universities and secondary schools throughout China. The Council has placed over 200 teachers, making it one of the U.S.'s largest non-religious providers of teachers to China.

Cross-Cultural Solutions

www.crossculturalsolutions.org

Cross-Cultural Solutions offers short-term and long-term programmes that give volunteers from all over the world the opportunity to come face to face with global issues and become part of productive solutions. CCS has close partnerships with social service pioneers in host countries. The focus of CCS's work is health care, education and social development.

Friends of World Teaching

www.fowt.com

Friends of World Teaching helps teachers find jobs around the world. Friends of World Teaching works with English-speaking schools and colleges throughout the world that offer employment opportunities to American and Canadian teachers. There are some student teaching programmes as well.

Global Routes
www.globalroutes.org
Global Routes is a tax-exempt, non-profit, non-governmental, non-sectarian organization whose aim is to strengthen the global community. It has designed community-service/cross-cultural-exchange programmes that bring people with different world-views together.

i-to-i
www.i-to-i.com
School and agency that provides TEFL training and manages extensive volunteer placements around the world (specialising in South and Central America and Asia). The agency provides accommodation, travel and support in-country. If you have never taught, it also offers courses for trainee-teachers.

India Literacy Project
www.ilpnet.org
India Literacy Project is a US-based non-profit, volunteer organization that focuses on literacy in India. Its aim is to empower every individual they serve with functional literacy and an understanding of their basic rights and responsibilities. India Literacy Project's goal is 100% literacy in India.

Intl. Foundation for Ed. & Self-help
www.ifesh.org
The International Foundation for Education and Self-Help (IFESH) was established as a non-governmental, nonprofit, charitable organization. IFESH aims to reduce hunger and poverty, empower people through literacy, train and place the unskilled and unemployed in jobs, provide preventive and basic health care to individuals in need, deal with population and environment problems, develop employment through economic development activities, foster cultural, social, and economic relations between Africans and Americans, particularly African Americans, and others.

International Rescue Committee
www.intrescom.org
International Rescue Committee was founded in 1933. The IRC is a nonsectarian, voluntary organization that provides relief, protection and resettlement services for refugees and victims of oppression or violent conflict throughout the world.

Intl. Schools Internship programme

www.tieonline.com

A TIE subscription gives you immediate access to the most prominent schools looking for staff: from 90 to 150 schools are always on the Job Ads web page. And the TIE Resume Bank means over 200 headmasters of International schools can access your file; and from there they can contact you through email, phone, your website, etc. Schools can, and often do, change their vacancies weekly at so you can be the first to know when a vacancy in the country you want opens up!

Laubach Literacy

www.laubach.org/home.html

Laubach Literacy Action (LLA), the U.S. programme Division of Laubach Literacy, is the largest volunteer-based literacy organization in the United States. They provide a full range of literacy services to more than 175,000 students annually through more than 1,000 local member programmes, 45 state organizations. Instruction is provided by a national network of more than 80,000 volunteer trainers and tutors .

Literacy Volunteers

www.literacyvolunteers.org

Literacy Volunteers of America, Inc. has served adults at the lowest levels of literacy and their families since 1962, and has assisted more than half a million people to acquire literacy skills. LVA offers a professionally designed and field-tested workshop that enables volunteers to tutor adults in English for speakers of other languages. After being matched with an adult learner or a small group of learners, tutors receive regular support and opportunities for additional training through the local LVA affiliate.

National Adult Literacy Database

www.nald.ca

The National Adult Literacy Database Inc. (NALD) is a federally incorporated, non-profit service organization which fills the crucial need for a single-source, comprehensive, up-to-date and easily accessible database of adult literacy programmes, resources, services and activities across Canada. It also links with other services and databases in North America and overseas.

PeaceCorps

www.peacecorps.org

As an English teaching volunteer, you will help expand the horizons and opportunities of students and teachers alike in Peace Corps' largest programme. There is no other experience like helping a middle school, secondary school, or university. More than 7,000 Peace Corps volunteers are serving in 76 countries. They are working to bring clean water to communities, teach children, help start new small businesses, and stop the spread of AIDS. Since 1961, more than 161,000 Americans have joined the Peace Corps, serving in 134 nations.

VolunteerMatch

www.volunteermatch.org

VolunteerMatch, ImpactOnline's main service, uses the power of the Internet to help individuals find volunteer opportunities posted by local non-profit and public sector organizations.

Volunteers in Asia

www.volasia.org

VIA is a private, non-profit, non-sectarian organization whose aim it is to increase understanding between the United States and Asia. Its Volunteer Programs in Asia have provided young Americans with an opportunity to work and live within an Asian culture while meeting the needs of Asian host institutions since 1962.

VSO (Voluntary Service Overseas)

www.vso.org.uk

The VSO is one of the biggest and best-known of the volunteer agencies. It works in over 70 countries around the world, with a current majority of postings to China and Africa. The VSO offers volunteers a complete package, including basic training (volunteers are expected to have a degree or be experienced TEFL teachers), airfares and, importantly, in-country support centres.

VSO Canada

www.vsocan.com

People are what VSO Canada is all about – and you just might be one of them. VSO's people share their skills in developing countries.

WorldTeach

www.worldteach.org

WorldTeach is a non-profit, non-governmental organization based at the centre for International Development at Harvard University which provides opportunities for individuals to make a meaningful contribution to international education by living and working as volunteer teachers in developing countries.

Gap Year

Gap-year travel (huge in the UK, unknown in the USA) is a way for students to take a year out and travel before settling down to their studies at university, often working as a volunteer (and teaching English is a popular option). The needs and expectations of both sides (agency and volunteer) are very different for gap year compared to a qualified teacher taking a career break or travelling, so there are agencies that specialise in this work. For information about working in your gap year, visit these websites:

The gap year company	www.gapyear.com
GAP Activity projects	www.gap.org.uk
Gap Challenge	www. world-challenge.co.uk

WORKING FOR YOURSELF

Whether you're working for a school or you just want to have enough money to stay living in a country, you could consider giving private lessons which will often be teaching one-to-one. It might be teaching the neighbour's kids or it could be the more lucrative business person who needs English for their job. Ask around to find out what the going rate is for private lessons. A great many teachers will do this as cash-in-hand and avoid the taxman but be aware that this is probably illegal.

It's advisable to draw up a mini-contract with your student(s). In some cultures attitudes to time-keeping are laid-back, so you may want to agree that if they are late for your class you won't extend the lessons to make up for their lack of punctuality. Some students may also think that if they fail to show up for a lesson you will make up the class another time so be clear about how much cancellation notice is required – 24 hours is probably reasonable. However, teaching privately is not only a good way to make extra cash but also a good way to meet people. Some teachers even do language swaps where you teach the student English for an hour and in return they teach you their language.

More websites and contacts

Good Places To Start

Dave's ESL Café
www.eslcafe.com

EFLweb
www.eflweb.com

English Teaching Professional
magazine
www.etprofessional.com

ESL Magazine
www.eslmagazine.com

IATEFL
www.iatefl.org

Internet TESL Journal
www.aitech.ac.jp/~iteslj

Linguistic Funland
www.linguistic-funland.com

Modern English Teacher magazine
www.onlineMET.com

Randall's ESL Cyber Listening Lab
www.esl-lab.com

TESL
www.tesl.com

TESOL organisation

Web Directories

These sites include directories of useful websites – a good place to start looking
for materials or other information online.

Business English Links for ESL
www.geocities.com/kurtracy/

English as a Second Language Page
www.rong-chang.com/

English as a Second/Foreign
Language for Kids
www.eslkid.com/

English Grammar Links for ESL
Students
www.gl.umbc.edu/~kpokoy1/gramm
ar1.htm

English Language Teaching Web
(ELTWEB)
www.eltweb.com/

ESL Café's Web Guide
www.eslcafe.com/search/index.html

ESL Forum
www.eslforum.net/

ESLdirectory.com
www.esldirectory.com/

GlobalStudy
www.globalstudy.com

Internet TESL Journal web directory
www.iteslj.org

Australian TESOL Websites Page
www.tesol.org.au/links.htm

English Language Teaching &
Learning Resources
www.bernieh.com.ar/

Bilingual and ESL Education Related
Resources
http://jan.ucc.nau.edu/~jar/BME.html

Carnegie Library's ESL/EFL Links
www.carnegielibrary.org/subject/education/esl.html

CATESOL's ESL Resources
www.catesol.org/resource.html

Online Resources for ESL Students and Teachers
www.clpccd.cc.ca.us/cc/maj/lahum/esl/resources.html

Bilingual / ESL Resources
www-rcf.usc.edu/~cmmr/BEResources.html

General English Links
www.englishnetlinks.homestead.com

ESL Webring
www.eslwebring.com

ESL-EFLworld Directory
www.esl-eflworld.com/

ESLoop
www.esloop.org/

IATEFL's BEsig – Links Page
www.besig.org/pages/links.htm

JALT Web Links
Http://jalt.org/jalt_e/main/materials_link/linkster.php

Teacher Associations

Almost every country has its own teacher association (often with many regional groups and smaller special-interest groups too!). These all help to provide information, news, support and newsletters (with the latest job opportunities). The two biggest groups are IATEFL and TESOL. Both have regional groups.

American Council on the Teaching of Foreign Languages (ACTFL)
www.actfl.org

Asociación De Profesores de Inglés de América Latina
www.aplial.net

Association for the Advancement of Computing in Education (AACE)
www.aace.org

Australian Council for TESOL Associations
www.tesol.org.au

Arizona-TESOL
www.az-tesol.org

BASELT – British Association of State English Language Teaching
www.baselt.org.uk

BC TEAL – British Columbia Teachers of English as an Additional Language
www.vcn.bc.ca/bcteal/

British Institute of English Language Teaching (BIELT)
www.bielt.org

Business English Special Interest Group of IATEFL
www.besig.org

California TESOL
www.catesol.org

Carolina TESOL
www.intrex.net/cartesol/

CASLT – Canadian Association of Second Language Teachers
www.caslt.org

English Language Teachers Contacts Scheme (ELTECS)
www.britishcouncil.org/english/eltecs/

EUROCALL – European Association for Computer Assisted Language Learning
www.hull.ac.uk/cti/eurocall.htm

Fukuoka JALT
www.kyushu.com/FukuokaJALT.html

Georgia TESOL
www.gatesol.org

IATEFL – International Association of Teachers of English as a Foreign Language
www.iatefl.org.uk

Indiana TESOL
www.intesol.org

JALT Testing & Evaluation Special Interest Group
www.jalt.org/test/

Japan Association of College English Teachers (JACET)
www.jacet.org

Japan Association of Language Teaching (JALT)
www.jalt.org

JETAA – The Japan Exchange and Teaching Alumni Association
www.jet.org

Korea Teachers of English to Speakers of Other Languages (KOTESOL)
www.kotesol.org

MIDITESOL – MidAmerica Teachers of English to Speakers of Other Languages
www.midtesol.org

Michigan TESOL
www.mitesol.org

NATECLA – National Association for Teaching English and other Community Languages to Adults
www.natecla.org.uk

Oregon TESOL
www.ortesol.org

TESOL – Teachers of English to Speakers of Other Languages
www.tesol.edu

TESOL Greece
www.tesolgreece.com

TESOL Spain
www.tesol-spain.org

TESOL Ukraine
www.tesol-ua.org

The Computer Assisted Language Instruction Consortium
www.calico.org

BALEAP – British Association of Lecturers in English for Academic Purposes
www.baleap.org.uk

English Language Teachers' Associations of Stuttgart and Frankfurt/Main, Germany
www.eltas.de

TESL Canada
www.tesl.ca

Schools

The web provides almost too much information about schools: almost every school has a website and it can be hard to compare them. Use one of these directories to help select a school according to type of course, level, experience and location.

ApplyESL.com
www.applyesl.com

Global Study
www.globalstudy.com

ESL Directory
www.esldirectory.com

Language Courses Comparison
www.languagecourse.net

eduPASS: US schools
www.edupass.org/english

Study in the USA
www.studyusa.com

Accredited schools in the UK
www.101schools.co.uk

Abracadebra ESL: Canadian schools
www.abracadabraesl.com

American Cultural Exchange
www.cultural.org/map.htm

Canadian Association of Private Language Schools
www.capls.com

Directory of ESL Programme Websites Around the World
www.globalstudy.com/esl/

Education and Homestay in New Zealand
www.studentstay.com

EF Education: chain of schools around the world
www.ef.com

EFL Directory
www.europa-pages.co.uk/uk/tefl.html

Study in the USA
www.studyusa.com

International Language Schools
www.aspectworld.com

GotoEd – Study English Abroad (outside the US)
www.gotoed.com

go2study
www.go2study.com/english/index.htm

Hyper Study: Australia and New Zealand
www.hyperstudy.com

TESL courses in Thailand
www.langserv.com

Bookshops

Argentina
KEL
www.ediciones-kel.com

SBS
www.sbs.com.ar

Brazil
Disal
www.disal.com.br

Liv. Martins Fontes
www.martinsfontes.com.br

Special Book Services
www.sbs.com.br

Chile
Books and Bits S.A.
www.booksandbits.cl

SBS
www.sbs.cl

Croatia
Algoritam
www.algoritam.hr

Czech Republic
Bohemian Ventures
www.venturesbooks.com

Mega Books International
www.megabooks.cz
Nakladatelstvi Fraus
www.fraus.cz

Denmark
English Center
www.englishcenter.dk

Egypt
Middle East Observer
www.meobserver.com.eg

Estonia
Accendo
www.accendo.ee

Allecto Bookshop
www.allecto.ee

Finland
The Academic Bookstore
www.akateeminen.com

France
Attica
www.attica-langues.com

Germany
Bookshop Stäheli Ltd.
www.staehelibooks.ch

Greece
Kosmos Floras Bookshops
www.floras.gr

Ireland
International Books
www.interbooksirl.com

Italy
Overseas Book Service
www.overseasbookservice.com

Japan
English Resource
www.englishresource.com

Nellie's Group
www.nellies.co.jp

Sanseido Bookstore
www.books-sanseido.co.jp

Korea
Kungman Book Center
www.kyobobook.co.kr

Kyobo Book Centre
www.kyobobook.co.kr

Mexico
Delti Bookstore
www.delti.com.mx

Russia
CenterCom
www.centercom.ru

Slovakia
Slovak Ventures
www.venturesbooks.com

Slovenia
DZS
www.dzs.si

Sweden
The English Book Centre
www.engbookcen.se

The Uppsala English Bookshop
www.ueb.se

Switzerland
Bergli Books
www.bergli.ch

Staeheli
www.staehelibooks.ch

Hans Stauffacher
www.stauffacher.ch

Taiwan
Caves Educational Training
www.cettw.com

UK
BEBC
www.bebc.co.uk

Cambridge International Book Centre
www.eflbooks.co.uk

English Book Centre
www.ebcoxford.co.uk

English Language Bookshop
http://elb-brighton.seekbooks.co.uk

KELTIC
www.keltic.co.uk

LCL International Booksellers
www.lclib.com

USA
Alta Book Center
www.altaesl.com

Delta Systems Co. Inc.
www.delta-systems.com

World of Reading, Ltd.
www.wor.com

Magazines

Magazines and journals are a teacher's best friends; they can provide practical information, lesson-plans and photocopiable material as well as a forum for technical discussions and analysis of methodology.

EL Gazette
www.elgazette.com

English Teaching Professional
www.etprofessional.com

ESL Magazine
www.eslmag.com

Hands-on English
www.handsonenglish.com/

IT's magazines
www.its.com

Language Magazine
www.languagemag.com

Mary Glasgow Magazines
www.link2english.com

Modern English Digest
www.ModernEnglishDigest.com

Modern English Teacher
www.onlineMET.com

Spotlight
www.spotlight.de

TESOL Journal
www.tesol.org/pubs/magz/tj.html

Publishers

ABAX ELT Publishers
www.abax.co.jp

Adams & Austen Press Publishers
www.aapress.com.au

Alta Book Center Publishers
www.altaesl.com

Barron's
www.barronseduc.com/english-language-arts.html

Beaumont Publishing
www.beaumont-publishing.com

Cambridge University Press
www.cup.cam.ac.uk

Crown House Publishing
www.crownhouse.co.uk

Delta Publishing
www.deltabooks.co.uk

Dymon Publications
www.dymonbooks.com

DynED International
www.dyned.com

Encomium Publications, Inc.
www.encomium.com

Express Publishing ELT Books
www.expresspublishing.co.uk

Full Blast Productions
www.fullblastproductions.com

Garnet Education
www.garneteducation.com

Georgian Press
www.georgianpress.co.uk

Griffith Books
www.griffith-books-ltd.sagenet.co.uk

HarperCollins Publishers
www.harpercollins.com

Heinemann
www.macmillaneducation.com

Heinle & Heinle Thomson Learning
www.heinle.com

Hodder and Stoughton
www.madaboutbooks.com

Houghton Mifflin
www.hmco.com

JAG Publications
www.jagpublications-esl.com

John Benjamins Publishing
www.benjamins.com/jbp/index.
html

Longman English language Teaching
www.longman-elt.com

Macmillan English
www.macmillanenglish.com

Marshall Cavendish ELT
www.mcelt.com

New Readers Press
www.newreaderspress.com

Oxford University Press
www.oup.co.uk

Peter Collin Publishing
www.bloomsbury.com/reference

Pro Lingua Associates
www.ProLinguaAssociates.com

Publishing Choice
www.publishingchoice.com

Richmond Publishing
www.richmondelt.com

Summertown Publishing
www.summertown.co.uk

The McGraw-Hill Companies
www.mhhe.com/catalogs/hss/esl/

Prentice Hall Regents
www.phregents.com

Addison-Wesley
www.awl.com

Conferences

There are thousands of conferences, shows and lectures around the world each year: every association has its own. The biggest are run by IATEFL (www.iatefl.org.uk) and TESOL (www.tesol.org). Use one of these sites that catalogues them all.

ELT Events Calendar in Japan
http://eltcalendar.com

TESOL Online's Conference Calendar
www.tesol.org/isaffil/calendar

Discussion and Mailing Lists

Discuss ideas and chat with colleagues and peers about materials, courses, schools or work – these discussion boards and emailing lists are dedicated to ELT.

Sign-up for TESL Mailing Lists
www.linguistic-funland.com/tesllist.html

Bulletin Board for EFL teachers working in Germany
http://pub95.ezboard.com/belt.html

CALLNews mailing list
http://listserv.cddc.vt.edu/mailman/listinfo/callnews

ELTASIA-L mailing list for ESL teachers in Asia
http://eltasia.com/

English Teaching Professional – discussion forum
www.etprofessional.com

ESL Café's Discussion Center for Teachers
www.eslcafe.com/discussion/#teacher

JALTTALK – Japan
www.jalt.org/jalt_e/main/jaltcall_main.shtml

Discussion Forums for Teachers
www.eslpartyland.com/tdisc.htm

Modern English Teacher – discussion forum
www.onlineMET.com

NETEACH-L – using technology in the classroom
www.ilc.cuhk.edu.hk/english/neteach/main.html

TESL-L Discussion List
www.hunter.cuny.edu/~tesl-l/

The ESL/Language ChatBoard
www.teachers.net/mentors/esl_language/

Free-ESL Discussion Forums
www.free-esl.com/teachers/forums/default.asp

Lesson Plans
Lesson plans are an essential part of every teacher's kit – trying to make teaching academic subjects such as grammar interesting, relevant to the student and easy to understand. The web has masses of free lesson plans that you can download and use as a basis for your own work. Try these sites for ideas and free plans.

EFL4U Lesson Plans
www.efl4u.com

ESLFLOW
www.eslflow.com

ESL Classroom Handouts
www.englishclub.net/handouts

Ideas for the ESL Classroom
www.eslcafe.com/ideas

ESL Teachers Guide
http://humanities.byu.edu/elc/
Teacher/TeacherGuideMain

Karin's ESL PartyLand
www.eslpartyland.com/teach3.htm

askERIC Lesson Plans
http://ericir.syr.edu/Virtual/Lessons

Games in ESL Classroom
http://eslsv001.esl.sakuragaoka.ac.
jp/teachers/BR/games/Games.html

Free Instant Lessons
www.english-to-go.com

English Lessons
www.nwrel.org/sky/

PIZZAZ!
http://darkwing.uoregon.edu/
~leslieob/pizzaz.html

TEFL Farm
www.teflfarm.com

TEFL.net
www.tefl.net

Lessons and Lesson Plans from The Internet TESL Journal
http://iteslj.org/Lessons/

Boggle's World ESL Lesson Plan Archive
http://bogglesworld.com/lessons/
archive.htm

Bradley's Worksheets
www.bradleys-english-
school.com/worksheets/nfindex.html

Free English Lessons
www.cerbranetics.com/english.html

Churchill House School of English Lanuage
www.churchillhouse.com/english/
downloads.html

CNN Newsroom Daily Classroom
http://Learning.turner.com/
newsroom/index.html

Free Lesson
www.english-to-go.com/english/

ESL Games and Activities
www.etanewsletter.com/games.htm

Teachers Teaching Teachers
www.etni.org.il/teacteac.htm

Activities for Summer School ESL
http://everythingesl.net/lessons/
summerschool_esl.php?ty=print

Classroom ESL Games
http://genkienglish.net/games.htm

Classroom Materials

Wordsmyth Glossary Maker
www.wordsmyth.net/foundry/
glossary.html

Wordsmyth Vocabulary Quiz
Generator
www.wordsmyth.net/foundry/
vocabquiz.shtml

Course for Adults
http://iteslj.org/Lessons/Vorland-
4units/

Crosswords and Word Searches for
Young Children
http://abcteach.com/EasyPuzzles/
kidsTOC.htm

Boggle's World
http://bogglesworld.com/

Community ESOL
www.communityesol.org.uk/

EFL Club Resource Box
www.eflclub.com/9resourcebox/
resourcebox.html

What's Wrong – Intensive Reading
http://esl.about.com/homework/esl/li
brary/lessons/nblwrong.htm

Grammar: Nature and Teaching
www.gabrielatos.com/Grammar.htm

Pronunciation: /r/ and /l/
www.csulb.edu/~linguag/ali/r_and_l.
html

Word Search Factory
www.schoolhousetech.com/
wordsearch.html

Classroom Materials Generators
www.teach-
nology.com/web_tools/materials/

Free handouts for EFL teachers
www.handoutsonline.com/

Simple English Grammar Exercises
www.theenglishprofessor.com/freewo
rksheets.htm

Teaching Tips and Ideas

If you're faced with your first class or if you are stuck for ideas after teaching the same subject to the thousandth student, these sites can help with fresh ideas and tips.

75 ESL Teaching Ideas
http://iteslj.org/Techniques/
Houston-TeachingIdeas.html

English Teaching Professional
magazine
www.etprofessional.com

Tips for Teachers
http://2merediths.org/esl/
teachertips.htm

Conversation starters for students
www.languageimpact.com/articles/rw
/conv_starters.htm

Teacher's Tips
www.developingteachers.com/tips/cu
rrenttip.htm

FAQ about Teaching ESL Students
www.fis.edu/eslweb/esl/students/
teanotes/

Forty Helpful Hints & Tips
www.handsonenglish.com

Hints and Pointers
http://genkienglish.net/general.htm

Practical Teaching Ideas on ESL
www.ncte.org/teach/esl.shtml

Survival Guide for New Teachers
www.ed.gov/pubs/survivalguide/

Tips for Teaching Grammar
www.ateg.org/grammar/tips.htm

Travel advice
www.1000traveltips.org
www.gapyear.com
www.goabroad.com
www.globetrotters.co.uk
www.journeywoman.com
www.lonelyplanet.com
www.roughguides.com
www.mapsworldwide.co.uk
www.timeout.com
www.vtourist.com
www.worldtimeserver.com

Official travel advice
British Foreign and Commonwealth office
www.fco.gov.uk

British passport enquiries
www.ukpa.gov.uk

US Department of State
www.travel.state.gov

NHS Direct
www.knowhow.co.uk

Emailing & cybercafés
Cybercafes.com
Visit before you go to find your local cybercafé – you'll be able to keep in touch with friends and family cheaply and quickly by emailing them while you're away. This website contains a list of over 4,000 Internet cafés around the globe.

Visas
Visas for Australia
www.australia.org.uk

Visas for USA
www.usembassy.org.uks

Finances
Mastercard
www.mastercard.com/atm

Visa
www.visa.com/pd/atm

American Express
www.americanexpress.com

Currency Conversion
www.xe.com

Western Union Money Transfer
www.westernunion.com

Travel health
National Centre for Disease Control
www.cdc.gov/travel

Travel health
www.tmvc.com.au/info10.html

TripPrep
www.tripprep.com

World Health Organization
www.who.int/ctd

Travel Agencies

Ebookers
www.ebookers.com

Expedia
www.expedia.com

STA Travel
www.statravel.co.uk

Trailfinders
www.trailfinders.co.uk

Intl Student Travel
www.istc.org

Studenttravel.com
www.studenttravel.com

Thomson travel
www.austravel.com

Ferry operators and ports

Brittany Ferries
www.brittanyferries.com

Hoverspeed
www.hoverspeed.co.uk

P&O Stena Line
www.posl.com

Stena Line
www.stenaline.co.uk

Bus

Buslines (Australia)
www.buslines.com.au

Greyhound (USA)
www.greyhound.com

Ticabus (Central America)
www.ticabus.com/Eindex/htm

Train

BudgetTravel
www.budgettravel.com

EuroRailways
www.eurorailways.com

Public Transport (in North America)
www.geocities.com/capitolhill/5355/

Australian Train Routes
www.gsr.com.au

RailServe
www.railserve.com

TrainWeb
www.trainweb.com/indiarail

Insurance abroad

When planning to travel abroad, you should you have adequate health insurance. With so many different types of coverage available, it can be very confusing deciding which plan is right for you. Here's what to look for.

Don't leave home without your E111

All European Union citizens are entitled to the same level of medical care in any other country of the EU as they would receive at home. To secure this coverage as a UK citizen, you must obtain form E111 from the Department of Health and Social Security before you leave the UK.

If you plan to stay for more than a few months, you should check what your local social security contributions entitle you to and decide whether you need to take out a private health care scheme. A private scheme gives you more flexibility about where you are treated, but you should check carefully to find out exactly what your coverage is. It is also possible to obtain coverage for repatriation in a real emergency.

Health Insurance: Home Country Coverage

This section will be of particular importance to citizens of the US (and other countries that do not have a good, free, state-funded health service) who typically have their own private health and medical insurance polices.

For US citizens, if you already have strong benefits at home, it is wise to double-check what exactly is covered while you are out of the country. Most health plans limit coverage to a maximum of 30 or 60 days outside the States, and HMOs and PPOs will likely impose severe – out of network – penalties for all but the most basic emergency care. More importantly, you will want to ensure you have 24 hour access to emergency evacuation if you are sick or hurt in an area where quality care is not available. For those over 65, Medicare will not cover treatment outside the U.S. If you do not have any domestic coverage, travel insurance is a must. Once you have answered these questions, you will need to know what benefits and policy provisions to look for in a travel medical plan.

Tax

It is most important to check whether or not the country you are going to has a reciprocal tax agreement with your home country.

If you are a UK national, you will get tax relief (even up to 100%) if you are out of the country for at least 365 days and do not stay in the UK for more than 62 consecutive days in the tax period. There is a difference between non-resident status and exemption from tax in the UK. If you are classed as a non-resident, you are not liable for tax on unearned income from abroad but you are still considered to be domiciled in the UK. To qualify as a non-resident you must work overseas for more than a full tax year without being in the UK for more than six months in that tax year or three months in each year if your stay abroad spans the tax year.

Many countries have agreements with the UK to prevent the double payment of tax. Credit against UK tax for payment already made abroad will be given if there is no such agreement. (See Inland Revenue form IR6 – Double Taxation Relief.)

When you are teaching abroad, it is important that you think about maintaining your UK social security payments so that you qualify for the state pension. You should get form N139 from the Department of Social Security (form SA29 if you are working in the EU).

Visas

It's always advisable to check the rules on working in a country if you are unsure. The quickest way to do this is to visit an embassy's website.

> ### MOVING ON
> At some point you're going to want to move on from your job to another school, town or country. It's worth noting that the world of TEFL is small so leave on good terms and avoid having to break a contract. Always get a reference from your employer that describes both your teaching and what you are like as an employee. This will be a useful document for the future when you apply for another TEFL job or for any other job.

Index